CEDEFOP

This handbook
has been prepared by
Jeremy Harrison
and
Henry McLeish

at the request of the European Centre for the Development
of Vocational Training (CEDEFOP), Berlin 1986

Published by:
European Centre for the Development
of Vocational Training,
Bundesallee 22, **D—1000 Berlin 15,**
Tel: (030) 884120; Telefax: 88412222; Telex: 184163 eucen d

The Centre was established by Regulation (EEC) No 337/75
of the Council of the European Communities

This publication is also available in the following languages:

ES   ISBN 92-825-6874-1
DE   ISBN 92-825-6875-X
GR   ISBN 92-825-6876-8
FR   ISBN 92-825-6878-4
IT   ISBN 92-825-6879-2
NL   ISBN 92-825-6880-6

Cataloguing data can be found at the end of this publication

Luxembourg: Office for Official Publications of the European Communities, 1987

Design: Rudolf J. Schmitt, Joachim Schmitt, Berlin

ISBN: 92-825-6877-6

Catalogue number: HX-46-86-581-EN-C

Printed in the FR of Germany

Young people in transition — the local investment

A handbook concerning the social and vocational integration of young people:
local and regional initiatives

Contents

Part three
Coordination and integration — A planned approach for administrators and practitioners at a local level

Part four
National and Community policies, mechanisms, guidelines, policy framework and proposals

Part five
Essential data

Introduction by CEDEFOP

Since it was recognized that the growing levels of youth unemployment were primarily due to neither cyclical nor demographic trends, and that there was likely to be a long-term problem, in both a quantitative and qualitative sense, relating to the insertion of young people in the labour market, there has been an emphasis in the Member States of the European Communities, and by the Community institutions, on the need for the development of a policy which looks at all aspects of the transition of young people from education to adult and working life simultaneously. It was recognized that separate approaches to their educational, vocational training, employment, social health and leisure time needs would not be conducive to success. This was perhaps most strongly expressed in the report[1] prepared by Professor Bertrand Schwartz for the French Prime Minister in 1981 and the succeeding programme involving the establishment of the *missions locales* in France. Similar initiatives followed in other countries.

At Community level, the second transition programme[2] from education to working life, involving the support of 30 pilot projects in all the Member States of the Community was based on a district approach. When this programme ends in 1987, it is probable that it will be replaced by a new programme, which will put considerable emphasis on the idea of 'local partnerships'. In the Commission's communications on the Vocational training of young people[3] and on International Youth Year[4] this emphasis on integrated local approaches was also cited.

CEDEFOP, therefore, believes that this handbook, which tries to give both practitioners and policy-makers some positive suggestions on how to provide the most effective range of opportunities to young people, and is based on the belief that these, to some extent must be planned and structured, as well as delivered, locally, comes at a very propitious time.

The methodology used in preparing the handbook is described, and there are many similarities to that which lead to the preparation of CEDEFOP's work on 'Planning of vocational preparation initiatives for unemployed young people' (1982) and its publication on *'Training for everyone'*, which will be published during 1987.

CEDEFOP is grateful to the participants in the working group, on whose experience the handbook is based, and to the authors, Jeremy Harrison and Henry McLeish, who collated a great deal of valuable information, and interesting viewpoints, into what is a very condensed, and we are confident, for the reader, attractive and logical framework.

Corrado Politi
Deputy Director

J. Michael Adams
Project Coordinator

November 1986

---

[1] *L'insertion professionnelle et sociale des jeunes,* La Documentation Française, septembre 1981.
[2] Council Resolution of 12 July 1982, OJ C 193 of 28. 7. 1982.
[3] Education and vocational training within the European Community, COM(85) 134 final of 29 March 1985.
[4] Memorandum by the Commission on International Youth Year, COM(85) 247 final of 1 July 1985.

Introduction

This handbook has been produced from the experiences and the ideas of a working group convened by CEDEFOP from six Member States of the Community. All the members of the group contributed freely descriptions of their activities, working and research papers, and examples of materials produced. In addition they attended meetings of the group at which they contributed to the design of this handbook and throughout which they debated the most difficult and contentious aspects of local coordination and integration of services. These meetings were divided between Berlin and the locations of initiatives themselves, where it was possible to see the reality behind the discussions. The group was particularly grateful to colleagues in Lorient, Cork, Randers and Chichester for the considerable effort they put into organizing meetings. Additional colleagues contributed by attending on one or two occasions to make special contributions. We are most grateful to all of them.

Group members who represented local initiatives

Bernard Durix
Mission locale de La Rochelle
Bonpland 15
rue des Fonderies
17000 La Rochelle
France
Tel: (046) 417525

Mirjam Depondt
Contactcentrum Onderwijs Arbeid (COA)
Limburg
Sint Pieterskade 7
6212 JV Maastricht
Netherlands
Tel: (043) 253012

Frits Glargaard
Teknisk Skole Randers
Vester Alle 26
8900 Randers
Denmark
Tel: (06) 426022

James Gorrie
Chichester College of Technology
Westgate Fields
Chichester
West Sussex PO19 1SB
England
Tel: (0243) 786321

Arthur Hammond
Manpower Services Commission
Exchange House, Worthing Road
Horsham
West Sussex RH12 1SQ
England
Tel: (0403) 50244 x 225

Richard Langford
Vocational Education Committee
Administrative Offices
Emmet Place
Cork
Ireland
Tel: (021) 93635

Jean-Luc le Clech
Mission locale de Lorient
44 Avenue de la Marne
56100 Lorient
France
Tel: (097) 214205

Roland Matzdorf
Ruhrwerkstatt
Kultur-Arbeit im Revier eV.,
Akazienstraße 107
4200 Oberhausen 1
Federal Republic of Germany
Tel: (0208) 803824 and 858424

Tom Mc Carthy
AnCO Training Centre
Rossa Avenue
Model Farm Road
Cork
Ireland
Tel: (021) 44377

Matty van Roozendaal
Contactcentrum Onderwijs Arbeid (COA)
Limburg
Sint Pieterskade 7
6212 JV Maastricht
Netherlands
Tel: (043) 253012

Christian Sondergaard
Handelsskolen in Randers
Minervavej 57
8900 Randers
Denmark
Tel: (06) 447222

Other participants from local initiatives who contributed to the work of the group in single meetings:

Ferd Gielen
Contactcentrum Onderwijs Arbeid (COA)
Limburg
Sint Pieterskade 7
6212 Maastricht
Netherlands
Tel: (043) 253012

Bryn Davies
Sussex Training Limited
Chichester College of Technology
Westgate Fields
Chichester
West Sussex PO19 1SB
England
Tel: (0243) 786321

Birgit Olbrich
Rurhwerkstatt
Kultur-Arbeit im Revier eV,
Akazienstraße 107
4200 Oberhausen 1
Federal Republic of Germany
Tel: (0208) 803824 and 858424

The work was also assisted by two members of the team coordinating, on behalf of the European Commission, the second EC programme on transition of young people from school to adult and working life:

Florence Gerard and Vagn Andresen
Ifaplan
Stadtwaldgurtel 33
5000 Köln 41
Federal Republic of Germany
Tel: (0221) 401061/64

and by

Gerard Sarazin and Michel Couteau
Délégation interministeriélle à l'insertion sociale et professionnelle des jeunes en difficulté
71, rue Saint-Dominique
75700 Paris
France
Tel: (01) 4555 9248

A great contribution was made by the representative of the Management Board of CEDEFOP, who attended many meetings:

Katerina Grekiotou
Ministry of Education
15 rue Mitropoleos
Athens 26
Greece
Tel: (01) 3231351

The project was administered and re-sourced from Cedefop by Michael Adams.

The contract was completed by
Jeremy Harrison
Henry McLeish
with the assistance of Arthur Harrison
for
J&S Harrison Associates Ltd
17 Station Road
Steeple Morden
Royston
Herts. SG8 ONW
England
Tel: (0763) 852871
        852070

We are also enormously grateful to the colleagues at CEDEFOP who provided us with the support and the resources essential to the exercise. Particularly important to a project of this kind were the interpreters, especially Annick Repellin.

Finally, the handbook was produced out of the papers provided by the group, and was fashioned by the discussions which took place in the group meetings, but responsibility for it rests with us. The finished product does not necessarily represent the views of the group. Collective views were not sought, and individual views have not been recorded. There will inevitably be parts of the handbook which some group members would have produced very differently, or not at all, though on the whole there was a wide measure of agreement.

Most importantly there was complete agreement on the central premise on which the handbook has been developed: policies and many ideas are often best developed on a national or even an international basis but, when they depend for their success on complex and sophisticated mixtures of guidance, education, training and work experience, they can only effectively be put into operation and delivered as a result of local planning and management.

Jeremy Harrison
Henry McLeish

January 1986

Glossary

Terms frequently used throughout the handbook

Young person:
anyone aged between 15 (or the school-leaving age, which differs from one Member State to another) and 26; some Member States work on narrower definitions, or do not use a precise definition.

Initiative:
an agency or a part of an agency with specific objectives and distinct methods of work.

Local:
an identifiable community, characterized either by formal boundaries, status as a *bassin d'emploi*, an acknowledged geographical or social identity, or the catchment area of a school or schools.

Coordination:
the organization of people or of institutions to contribute to the provision of a service for young people.

Integration:
the combination of techniques, methods, projects or programmes to provide for young people.

Small and medium-sized enterprises:
those with fewer than 500 employees.

Basic training:
training designed to identify abilities, provide experience of work, and a general level of knowledge about work itself, and a foundation upon which skills can be built.

Vocational training:
training for a particular skill or occupation.

Transition (from school to work):
the period covering the last two years of compulsory schooling up to the acquisition of a job (after basic and vocational training).

Information:
linked services designed to provide young people with access to facts on which they can make judgements and decisions

Advice:
linked services designed to provide young people with expert assistance in making these judgements and decisions, and, where necessary, with personal support and assistance with problems which cannot be solved by other means.

Important abbreviations

Denmark

EIFU:
Erhvervsintroducerende kurser for unge arbejdsledige
Introductory vocational courses for young unemployed people

EFG:
Erhvervsfaglig grunduddannelse
A scheme of alternating training, based on one-year school-based training, followed by two years of on-the-job training

France

ANPE:
Agence nationale pour l'emploi
National employment agency

AFPA:
Association pour la formation profession-nelle des adultes
National association for adult vocational training

CIO:
Centre d'information et orientation
Information and guidance centre

CEF:
Contrat emploi-formation
Employment-training contract

COAE:
Centre d'orientation et d'actions éducatives local
Centre for guidance and local educational initiatives

GRETA:
Groupement d'établissements
Grouping of institutions for continuing education and training
(Ministry of Education)

TUC:
Travaux d'utilité collective
Work of social and community value

Ireland

COMTEC:
Community training and employment consortia

AnCO:
An Chomhairle Oiliúna
Industrial Training Authority

VEC:
Vocational Education Committee

NMS:
National Manpower Service

YEA:
Youth Employment Agency

CERT:
Council for Education, Recruitment and Training for the Hotel and Catering Industry

ACOT:
An Chomhairle Oiliúna Talmhaíochta
Agricultural Training Authority

Netherlands

VWO:
Voorbereidend wetenschapzelijk onderwijs
Academic secondary school

HAVO:
Hoger algemeen voortgeget onderwijs
Higher general secondary school

MAVO:
Middelbaar algemeen voortgeget onderwijs
Intermediate secondary school

MBO:
Middelbaar beroepsonderwijs
Intermediate vocational education

LBO:
Lager beroepsonderwijs
Lower vocational education

United Kingdom

MSC:
Manpower Services Commission

YTS:
Youth Training Scheme

Using the handbook

The handbook has been constructed so that it can be used in different ways by readers with different practical needs, but who all have something of importance to learn from the experience of others who are

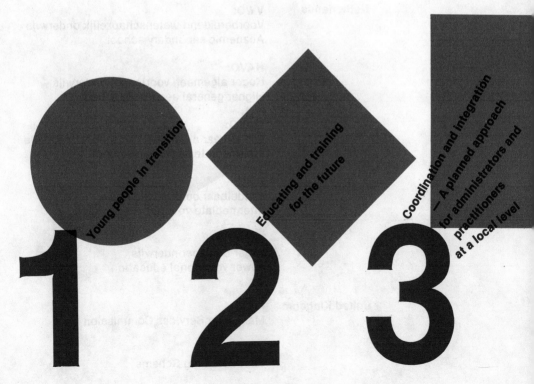

Young people in transition

Educating and training for the future

Coordination and integration — A planned approach for administrators and practitioners at a local level

1 2 3

— relating educational and training opportunities to local and individual needs,

— seeking fresh approaches to integrated services for young people trapped by unemployment, social and economic change, and frequently poor living conditions,

— conscious of the need to achieve the highest quality at the lowest cost.

It has been written from the experience and from the point of view of practitioners, of people whose job it is to construct initiatives and projects, rather than from that of officials whose job it is to devise national or regional programmes.

4 National and community policies mechanisms, guidelines, policy framework and proposals

5 Essential data

Use the handbook as

1
A guide

- Use it as a guide to ideas and techniques, not as a blueprint.

- Approaches which succeed in one Member State are most unlikely to be capable of being transplanted literally into another.

- But the problems and the essential needs of young people are very similar.

- The difficulties of integrating and co-ordinating the work of different agencies and institutions are essentially the same.

- We are all facing the same crisis of employment, and similar social dislocation caused by change.

2
A practica

- It sets out and analyses the ideas and the problems facing administrators and managers in local and national initiatives.

- It is an information source, an exchange of techniques.

manual

- It sets out to give direct help with the planning of objectives and the setting of boundaries and limits of action.

- It recognizes, argues and clarifies problems of principle and of a practical nature.

- It provides illustrations of good practice drawn from the activities of the members of the working group from which the handbook was produced.

- It provides an index list of references.

3 A starting point

- It is intended to provide a route to further advice and help, either through the contacts provided in Member States or through CEDEFOP itself.

- It is intended to provide a means by which expert and professional people in different agencies, institutions and disciplines can advance and improve the ways in which they combine and cooperate to provide services for young people in transition.

- It is a result of collaboration by a group of professionals prepared to share their knowledge freely. It is hoped that it will encourage others to do the same, on a bilateral or multi-lateral basis.

Young people in transition

Contents

Young people throughout the European Community face grave and unprecedented difficulties in finding jobs once they have completed compulsory education. It is widely understood that this has come about through a combination of structural and technological change in industry, which has tended to reduce the supply of unskilled and semi-skilled jobs, resulting in an oversupply of labour, reinforced in most Member States by very large numbers of young people leaving school in recent years.

This handbook is a guide — not a blueprint — for the many people throughout the Community who are concerned:

● to help bring young people themselves closer together in order to improve their prospects of successfully preparing for a future containing at least as much economic and social change as the present, and in order to help them live successfully despite the uncertainties and difficulties they face;

● to bring young people closer to the variety of institutions which are trying to help them, and to help those institutions organize what they do on a more efficient, sensitive and effective basis than is inevitably the case if they make no effort to coordinate what they do.

These issues are of great importance throughout the Community because:

- Young people bear to a disproportionate degree the hardship which results from mass unemployment — hardship which results in social and psychological difficulties as much as it does in financial and occupational problems.

- At international, national and local levels considerable, but often uncoordinated efforts are being made to improve the whole range of educational, training, advisory and social services available to young people in transition from school to adult and working life. Uncoordinated efforts of this kind, however well-directed they may be to the needs of young people in transition from school to adult and working life, are both less efficient, and less cost-effective than they would be if they were clearly related to each other, and at the same time based on common understandings of **local** needs and opportunities.

- Whenever the real needs of young people are carefully considered it becomes clear that they relate in a complex way to educational, vocational, social and personal problems. It is not always possible to separate these needs, and it is invariably better to make every effort to integrate solutions to them. Often it is not possible to achieve an effective solution for one problem without at the same time providing help with another.

This was emphasized by the European Commission in its Communication to the Council of Ministers, 'Vocational training policies in the European Communities in the 1980s'.[1]

'The idea of an integrated approach to development for the regions and local areas, including the training dimension, is gaining ground rapidly throughout the Community. Over the last few years, moreover, there has been a marked trend in some Member States to decentralize vocational training to the regional level of decision-making, so that it takes place closer to the point of need. This trend, though not common to all Member States, must be viewed alongside the growing concern to link training policies with wider social and economic strategy to regenerate disadvantaged regions.'

---

[1] COM (82) 637 of 21 October 1982.

The communication then went on to acknowledge some of the difficulties inherent in this approach:

'However, since generally education, training, employment and economic structures still tend to be organized on a compartmentalized basis, at national level in particular, the effective delivery of integrated operations still remains the ideal rather then practical reality in most cases.'

This reality has been largely accepted within Member States, and this handbook has been to a large extent prompted by the knowledge of particular attempts to do something about it.

Among those which are well-known at Community level (though not necessarily understood) are the *Missions locales* in France, the contact centres for education and work in the Netherlands, and the local arrangements for organizing the youth training scheme in the United Kingdom. These are all dealt with by example in this handbook, as are others, widely different from each other, but each consistent with an overall intention to coordinate the complex elements of training, education, work experience and advice and counselling which are essential components of any concerted programme for young people.

1.2. The local significance

At a local level the consequences of the changes in employers' needs for labour, and of the growing importance of the new technologies — both are components of education and of training programmes — have included considerable discussion and often confusion about the objectives of education and training, and the roles of the institutions which provide them.

In this handbook we have not concerned ourselves with debating the boundaries between education and training, but have taken an almost contrary point of view. We have accepted that doubt and confusion exist, as do legitimate and necessary debates which will, in some cases, result in much-changed definitions of objectives, methods and responsibilities.

We have concerned ourselves primarily with the period of change and uncertainty which currently exists, and which seems likely to persist for some considerable time.

The victims of this change are young people themselves — a disproportionate percentage of the unemployed and the insecurely employed, who, of course, form the larger group of those who bear the greatest weight of deprivation and uncertainty.

It is known that they rightly perceive themselves to be surplus to the needs of the labour market, at least for the time-being. They have no means of knowing if they will ever be needed. And if they are needed, they cannot know in what capacity.

They see themselves as being offered a range of activities the general effect of which is to remove them from the labour market whilst keeping them usefully occupied, and there are signs throughout the Community of them taking a critical view of the probable usefulness of many of the occupations on offer to them. They can legitimately ask:

(a)
Is this experience likely to be useful to them in their future careers? Does it provide them with knowledge, skills or experience which may help them respond to work opportunities if and when they arise?

(b)
Is it immediately useful, either to them as individuals, or to the communities in which they live?

A third and fourth series of questions which are inevitably, and perfectly reasonably asked are:

(c)
How are they expected to live? What will they be paid?

(d)
If work is a privilege accorded mainly to those who already enjoy many of the advantages in life, is there a good reason why those who are denied it through no fault of their own should be made to suffer financially as well as in terms of social and personal status and pride?

These are all difficult, and often unpleasant questions to have to attempt to answer. Frequently there are no good or complete answers.

This handbook is written from the point of view of people who comprehend these questions, who frequently ask them themselves, but who at the same time are committed to providing the best possible range of choices and opportunities, and who have taken the view that these questions must be faced and dealt with at a local level.

It is written for others who share that practical commitment.

1.3. National and local: some implications

Local coordination of any wide range of services for young people in transition is inherently difficult.

● Nationally-made policies, and the rules and practices of established national agencies and institutions are usually difficult to match with each other, and complex to apply to local circumstances.

● Resources are often provided at a national level, allowing little flexibility to take account of precise local needs.

● It is difficult, and can be expensive and time-consuming to discover what young people really want.

● Local agencies and institutions often have a history of rivalry and competition, and will not collaborate easily, even if they know how to.

The first step in overcoming some of these problems is simply to understand their relationship to each other.

For many practitioners one of the most useful tools in understanding both the difficulties of local coordination, and ways of overcoming those difficulties, is an awareness of how others are facing these problems.

This handbook has been put together on the basis of first-hand and practical examples because:

● although no one in the Community claims to have solved the problem of making the right provision in the most effective and the most cost-effective way at a local level, many are working hard at their own approaches; they have a great deal to communicate, and a great deal to learn from others;

● although the examples are different from each other in many respects (sometimes because they have grown from quite different roots, and sometimes because they have simply developed in different kinds of labour markets, and in very different social settings), they share common concern and attitudes to the difficulties which young people face, and they share a commitment to making a variety of people and resources work together.

European and national priorities are rarely in **conflict** with local realities, but matching them is always time-consuming, and often difficult . . . .

European Community and national priority

| YOUNG PEOPLE NEED THE BEST EDUCATION, TRAINING & GUIDANCE IF THEY ARE TO SURVIVE AND COMPETE | MONEY BEING SPENT NEEDS TO BE SEEN TO BE ACHIEVING THE BEST RESULTS AT THE BEST PRICE |

Local implication

Only at a local level can unqualified and poorly-qualified young people make real choices, and influence what is provided.

The best results will be achieved by coordinated efforts on the part of agencies and institutions working together in the context of local resources and local needs.

Laws and programmes developed at a national level can only be relevant, and therefore fully effective, if every chance is taken to relate them to local needs and opportunities.

But

though this is easy to say,
● it is far from easy to find out what young people want;
● there must be some effective means of relating needs and preferences in vocational matters to those in other fields, like housing, personal problems, drugs, etc.

But

this may be difficult to achieve because:
● there is no tradition of collaboration;
● often there are no useful mechanisms to see that it happens;
● even when there are, it is difficult because real objectives and assumptions are not always shared — there may be rivalry.

But

if this is to be successful:
● there must be some understanding of how local labour markets work;
● national programmes have to be sufficiently flexible to allow for local delivery.

These are all difficulties and complications which the best initiatives accept, deal with and often turn to advantage.

1.4. National and local : seven initiatives

Seven initiatives from six Member States have been the focus of the work through which this handbook has been developed. Their experience has informed its approach, and illustrations of their work provide the basis for its analysis and its suggestions to other practitioners.

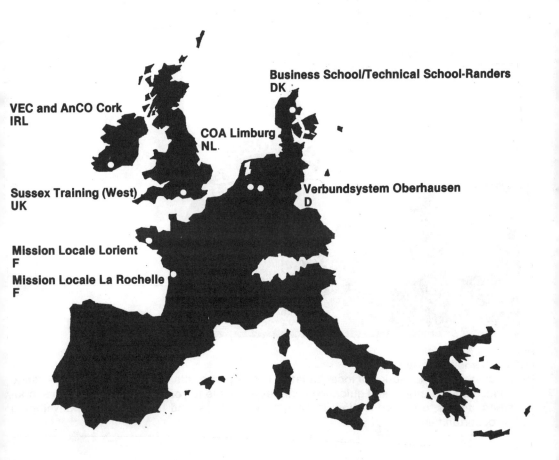

Business School/Technical School-Randers
DK

VEC and AnCO Cork
IRL

COA Limburg
NL

Sussex Training (West)
UK

Verbundsystem Oberhausen
D

Mission Locale Lorient
F

Mission Locale La Rochelle
F

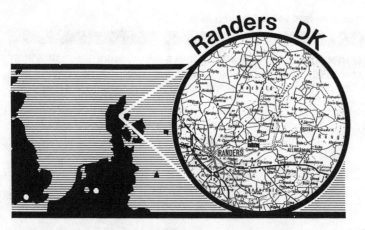

Business School/Technical School — Randers, DK

The cooperation between the Business School and the Technical School in Randers ensures the legal obligation which exists in Denmark to assist young people between the ages of 16 and 18 with their transition from school to work, even when they have left the compulsory schooling system.

The system of advice and counselling is provided in close collaboration with local social partners.

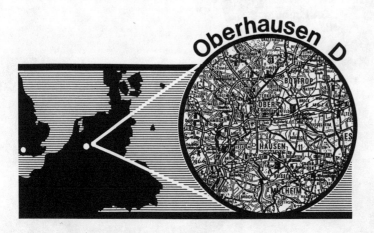

The Oberhausen network — D

The Oberhausen network is a local initiative in this part of the Ruhr coordinating the range of educational, training and guidance facilities available to young people who leave school and are unable to find education, training or workplaces, and finding ways of developing new opportunities.

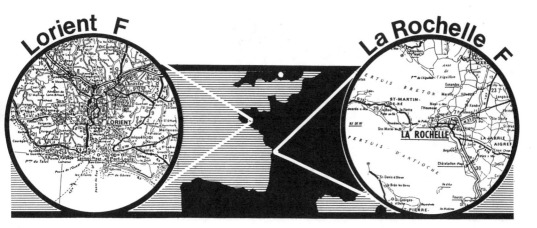

Missions locales for the transition of young people to adult and working life — Lorient and La Rochelle, F

The *Missions locales* in Lorient and La Rochelle are two examples of a network of 100 local centres placed in areas of high unemployment in France. They are the result of a collaboration on one level between the central government and local authorities, and on another between the social partners and a wide range of educational, training and social agencies. They provide a focus of advice and assistance for young people with any problems they experience, not just those directly connected with employment, and they also serve as catalysts and animators of new forms of provision for young people.

Cork Vocational Education Committee and AnCO, the Industrial Training Authority — IRL

The Vocational Education Committee, responsible for a high proportion of secondary and vocational education in the city, and AnCO, the Industrial Training Authority, which is responsible for a wide range of basic and specific vocational training programmes are taking the lead in coordinating services for young people. Apart from informal cooperation, which has developed over a number of years, they are both closely involved in the Comtec, which is designed to give a more formal authority to coordination.

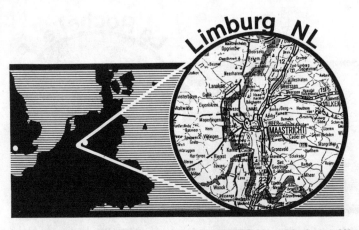

Contact Centre for Education and Work (COA) — Limburg, NL

The COA Limburg is part of a national network of contact centres set up on a provincial and local basis, to develop educational, training, work experience and guidance facilities for young people, and to help the providers of these services to coordinate their objectives and their activities.

Sussex Training (West) — Chichester, UK

Sussex Training (West) is a consortium established to ensure that the widest possible range of local employers involve themselves in providing training for young people under the Government's youth training scheme (YTS).

The initiative was promoted by, and is run from, the Chichester College of Technology, and is financed by the Manpower Services Commission (MSC).

The consortium covers South-West Sussex, and includes representatives of all social partners.

Note:
Fuller descriptions of these initiatives form the largest part of 'Part five: Essential data'.

These examples are of special value and interest because — despite their similarities of objectives — they are very **different** from each other in important respects:

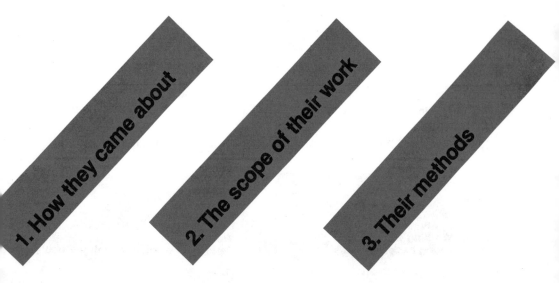

1. How they came about
2. The scope of their work
3. Their methods

1. How they came about

Some arose as part of national initiatives, or as a result of laws

> The *Missions locales* — F
> COA Limburg — NL
> Randers Business School/Technical School — DK

Others result from local initiative

> The Oberhausen Verbundsystem — D
> Sussex Training (West) — UK
> Cork VEC/AnCO — IRL

2. The scope of their work

They concentrate on:

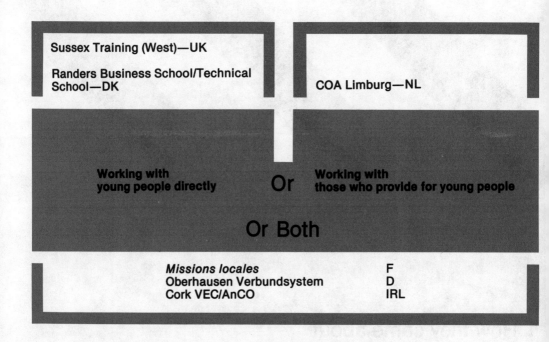

Sussex Training (West)—UK

Randers Business School/Technical School—DK

COA Limburg—NL

Working with young people directly

Or

Working with those who provide for young people

Or Both

Missions locales   F
Oberhausen Verbundsystem   D
Cork VEC/AnCO   IRL

3. Their methods

There are three **main** methods of work in use amongst the seven initiatives:

Four of them are focused mainly on one of the methods. (They all make use of the others from time to time). Three initiatives are specifically structured to employ all the methods.

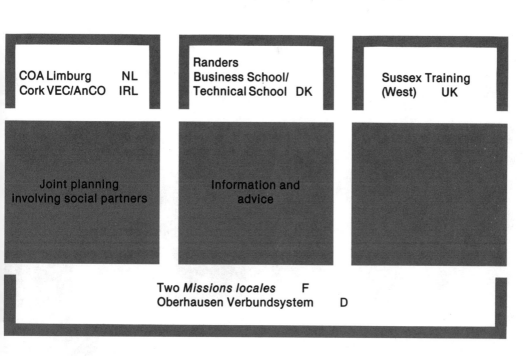

COA Limburg   NL
Cork VEC/AnCO   IRL

Randers
Business School/
Technical School DK

Sussex Training
(West)   UK

Joint planning
involving social partners

Information and
advice

Two *Missions locales*   F
Oberhausen Verbundsystem   D

Educating and training for the future

Contents

This section is intended as a practical aid to anyone who is trying to construct a means of providing good vocational education and training for young people — to anyone who is looking for ways of improving or extending an existing local system — to anyone who simply wants to compare their approaches with those of professionals in other Member States for purposes of planning or as material for training exercises.

It contains:

2.1. Boundaries and options

2.2. Issues and principles

2.1. Boundaries and options

It is rarely possible to transplant a complete initiative from one Member State to another. It is often impossible to transplant one successfully from one part of the same Member State to another. This handbook presents a variety of experiences which are intended to be treated not as blueprints, but as guides. They are aids to planning, not substitutes for it.

Successful local initiatives — particularly those which involve complex planning and coordination of different projects and resources must be built on an understanding of two kinds of boundaries:

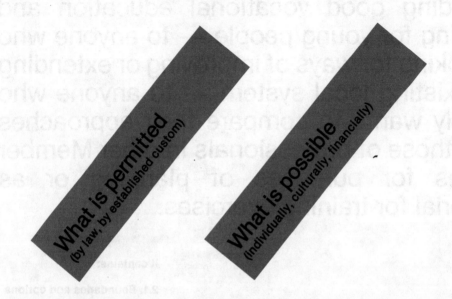

what is permitted
(by law, by established custom)

what is possible
(Individually, culturally, financially)

2.1.1. What is permitted

What is permitted varies very considerably from one Member State to another depending partly upon the attitudes and policies of governments, but also (and more importantly) on the tradition of law, and the accepted manner of government.

A visitor from one Member State to another once compared the country he was visiting to a third Member State: 'I have the impression that in this country everything is permitted unless it is specifically forbidden, whilst in ****** everything is forbidden unless it is specifically permitted.' That was an exaggeration, but it illustrated the difference between some systems where everything tends to be defined in terms of legislation, and others where legislation provides a framework, but many activities are ultimately governed either by precedent or by the decisions of State or semi-State agencies.

Other differences arise from the balance of executive responsibility between national and local authorities. This varies a great deal from one Member State to another, and in some cases the trend is towards greater centralization, and in other cases towards devolution of powers from the centre.

What is permitted may be governed by:

Law

Custom and practice

Collective agreements

State and semi-State agencies

2.1.2. What is possible

The best results from training (especially from basic training provided for young people with poor qualifications or with no qualifications at all) are invariably achieved by trainers who are capable of taking an open and optimistic view of their personal abilities.

The belief that **every young person has abilities and is capable of acquiring some skills** is essential.

● If a young person **appears** to have no abilities on which training can be based, this is almost certainly either because the **trainer** is unable to find them or because there are insufficient or inappropriate training resources available.

● Academic achievement (or lack of it) is not always a good guide to ability to learn skills in an adult, working environment.

● There are numerous examples of successful trainers demonstrating to young people that disadvantages (and even handicaps) need have no relevance to ability to train and to work. There are also instances of trainers showing young people how to convert apparent disadvantages into advantages.

Successful trainers are those who are able to work with each trainee as an individual:

Identifying abilities

Teaching skills

Finding a job

Labour market

Successful training programmes are those which are devised to match new ideas with accepted values, innovation with familiar ideas and methods — all within the bounds of what is permitted and what is possible.

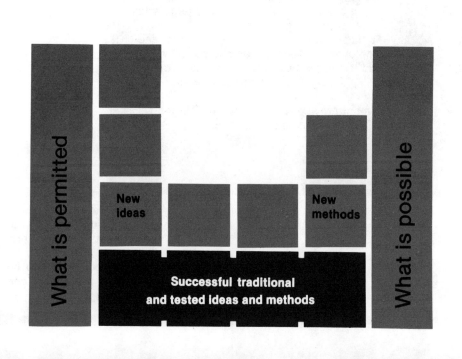

What is permitted

New ideas

New methods

Successful traditional and tested ideas and methods

What is possible

Successful training programmes are those which focus most effectively on **medium-term needs.**

Short-term needs
can usually be identified quite easily.
They are important, but are the easiest to satisfy.

Medium-term needs
Training is a medium-term activity focusing on **predictable** needs of workers and employers.
To keep the confidence of workers and employers it must be of short-term value and it must provide a flexible basis for adaptation to long-term changes.

It must provide a vocational foundation for the medium term.

Long-term needs
often appear important but they cannot reliably be predicted.
They are too distant to be clear. They are almost certain to change.

Successful local programmes focus on training needs and on social and personal needs. Young people can only learn effectively if their personal and social circumstances allow them to concentrate adequately. It may be of little value training a young person who has no home, and who may not be able to learn or work effectively as a result. A young person may need to be restored to full health before being able either to learn or to work.

What is possible also depends finally on the views which individuals, groups or agencies responsible for programmes take of an important range of issues affecting young people and their place in society, and on a number of principles about how they should be treated, and how they can be involved in determining their own futures.

2.2. Issues and principles

There are three groups of important considerations affecting the ways in which provision can be made for young people:

● the needs of young people themselves, how to decide what they are, and how to respond to them;

● the realities of achieving the best local results from national policies, and about reconciling national and local priorities;

● the benefits and the difficulties of bringing together and coordinating the efforts and the resources available from different agencies and institutions.

2.2.1. Young people's needs

Consultation
The first and most important question which must be asked about any education, training or social initiative is **'Does it provide what people need?'** The question appears to be simple, but it is not. How does one decide what people need? On the basis of what they say they need? On the basis of previous experience of what has satisfied others? On the basis of some scientific investigation or assessment? On the basis of guesswork? Or on the basis of first calculating what it is possible to provide, and then arguing its relevance? In reality adults frequently find reasons for failing to consult young people about their needs and preferences before they provide some service for them. This may be because they do not expect young people to have anything constructive to suggest.

It may be because they do not know how to consult young people, or which young people to consult. Also, there is something wrong with any education or training measure designed to help young people adapt themselves to a changing society, which is itself not sufficiently flexible to be responsive to changes which those who use it may need to make in it. There is something wrong with any educator or trainer who is unable to respond to the suggestions and criticisms of his or her students or trainees. Needs can neither be identified nor properly catered for unless this dialogue takes place.

Co-determination/self-management

Most experienced educators and trainers would go much further. They would argue that there are two powerful sets of reasons for proposing that young people concerned with programmes designed to help them make the transition from school to adult and working life should have every opportunity to **co-determine** what those programmes contain, and should also, as far as possible enter into **self-management** of their own participation in them.

The first reason is that by being involved and engaged in what they are learning, they are more likely to feel motivated to make good use of it, and to seek ways of making it better and more relevant to their needs and to those of other young people.

The second reason is that in a changing labour market and in social climates where young people are often insecure and at a disadvantage, independence, the ability to make decisions, and the ability to manage and control resources, and to protect them, are all vital components of personal and group development.

It is more common for people responsible for education and training to agree with these propositions than it is for them to put their beliefs into practice. It is much easier to train a young person in a particular skill and then to measure the efficiency with which he or she applies it, than it is to help a young person decide which skills to learn, allow him or her to take a leading role in planning the manner, the speed and the context in which learning will take place . . . and then to provide the training and measure the resulting achievement.

Social and material status

Unemployment among young people, and the extended period which large numbers of them are now having to spend in transitional activites (however beneficial) between school and adult employment, both create great personal and social stresses which are related to some degree to the fact that young people in these circumstances have no clear status in their communities, and very little material reward for what they do.

The young long-term unemployed

The problem is most acute for young people who are also long-term unemployed (which is generally taken to mean that they have been unemployed for a year or more). In their case the problems of status and identity which adult unemployed experience are compounded by the fact that they have never worked at all, and therefore have nothing to prove that they were ever of use. In many Member States they cannot call themselves, for instance, 'unemployed machinists', or 'unemployed office workers'. They are just 'unemployed', with no means of or proving that they are even 'employable'.

Young people in transitional activities

For them, the problems of identity are less acute, but they exist. The whole range of transitional activities — basic training, vocational preparation, work experience, intermediate enterprises — have been directed onto young people partly because labour markets have changed, and therefore training and education had to change, and partly because there is simply nothing else for them to do.

Are they trainees? . . . Yes, in a sense. But often they do not know what they are training for, or how long it will take.

Are they workers? . . . Some are, but not necessarily in what they consider to be real jobs.

46

Targeting

Governments, local authorities and even specialist agencies and organizations usually try to 'target' assistance on those who need it most. This is generally for financial reasons, but often for professional reasons. Targeting is difficult, complex and frequently inefficient — resulting in the neglect of people who need help or attention.

When the French *Missions locales* were designed, they were set up for 'young people in difficulty'. It was correctly assumed that young people who experienced problems in other aspects of their lives would find extreme difficulty in acquiring suitable education and training after the end of compulsory schooling, and would be at a great disadvantage in the employment market. However, the parallel assumption that young people who did not suffer from other difficulties would be able to organize their transition from school to adult life and work was not correct. In France, as in other Member States, people who were actually working with young school leavers and the young unemployed were confronted with the fact that most young people need some help, and many young people need a good deal of help. Moreover, and regardless of personal need, all young people were in need of information, advice and counselling about labour markets, and about social circumstances which have changed quickly and radically, and which are continuing to change. Well-organized, professionally coordinated ranges of educational, vocational and social options, accompanied by accurate information and good-quality advice and counselling, are precisely what young people in difficulty require. But they are equally vital to young people with no personal or social difficulties, but who also have to try to find career paths in difficult and confusing circumstances. Comprehensive, locally relevant initiatives should be **available** to all young people, because **any** individual young person may be in great need without necessarily appearing to be especially vulnerable, disadvantaged or deprived.

Provision for young people with special needs

The most important objective of trying to achieve coordination of educational, training and other services for young people is to ensure that they are able to be part of a mainstream of transition to working and adult life, whilst at the same time benefiting from the widest possible choice of personally appropriate opportunities. Young people need wide choice within a comprehensible and consistent framework. This principle clearly applies to young people with special needs. If they are dealt with entirely through special provision, they are brought up in a world peopled by others whose disadvantages and handicaps have become the most important aspects of them. If they are prepared for adult life and work in the same system as all young people, and as far as possible alongside them, then their handicaps and disadvantages can be acknowledged and catered for, but their abilities and their aspirations can be recognized and developed. Segregation of young people with special needs is often the easiest administrative option, but it serves to reinforce and preserve disadvantage, and to work against real equality of opportunity. When integration is adopted as a principle it allows specialist services to be provided where necessary, but encourages concentration on personal strengths and abilities rather than on weaknesses and disabilities.

Provision for young women

The issue of equal treatment of young women, and equal opportunity for them in education, training and the job market itself is one of the most important considerations in any national or local programme of education, training or information, advice and counselling. It represents a high priority in European Community policies and is considered of great importance by Member States. There is a great deal of disagreement, however, about how the objective of equal opportunity should be pursued. Whether it should be through measures of positive discrimination designed to correct past bias against women, or whether it should simply be pursued through complete equality of treatment on every occasion. The fact is that, while it is of great value to adopt principles and policies at a European level, it is of no great advantage to try to impose ideas about practice. Not only do the historical handicaps under which women have operated differ quite significantly between one Member State and another, but the contemporary circumstances in which equality of opportunity is being developed differ a great deal as well. There are clearly some instances where women will only develop their abilities to the full if they are given some chance to do it in relatively relaxed circumstances where they are not directly in competition with men. There are instances where special provision is necessary. There are other instances where special provision may be the most attractive and efficient way of organizing education or training, but where what is being learned is of no particular value outside the context in which it can be applied — many training courses are just as much concerned with ways of working with colleagues as they are with skills required to perform tasks. This is especially true in service industries.

The most important single considerations are:

● that all education, training and work experience should be conducted in circumstances where the importance of equality of opportunity is acknowledged and understood, and where instances of deliberate or accidental discrimination can be recognized and dealt with;

● that all young women should have access to individual and specialist advice (and where necessary counselling) to complement the comprehensive supply of information which is essential if young people are to make their own choices and decisions about their futures;

● that everyone involved in designing and administering initiatives offering complete equality of opportunity should understand that **nothing** will be completely effective until society as a whole **accepts** that damage is done by discrimination, and **demands** that equality be reflected in every aspect of life and work.

Information, guidance and counselling

If young people are to be equipped to find their way in job markets which are subject to considerable change and instability, the central objective of whatever is done must be to give them the information they require to understand local opportunities and circumstances, and to relate these to wider opportunities. If this cannot be done, one whole aspect of local coordination is entirely missed. There is then very little point in expending money and effort on providing good information services for young people unless a parallel effort is made to ensure that they have access to advice on how to interpret and use what they have acquired. There are three vitally important considerations attached to the provision of information and advice services:

- they must be as comprehensive as possible, enabling vocational and educational advice to be complemented with information and advice about other problems which would normally be dealt with separately, but act and interact on each other in young people's real lives;

- they must be, and must be seen to be, neutral, as far as possible; young people want to make their own choices, and cannot be expected to welcome attempts to impose choices upon them;

- to be successful they must be provided through whatever media and agencies young people themselves value and accept; above all they must make use of informal and traditional methods including friends, family and parents.

It is not possible to claim to be offering young people the means of making choices and achieving independence without making sure that they have the information on which to take decisions, and the advice and counselling they may need to enable them to be applied successfully. This is the central theme of this handbook.

National and local priorities

Since vocational training has become a subject for national policy-making in all Member States, and since training has become increasingly integrated with education and with educational resources, it has become commonplace for training measures to be defined and financed (at least in part) at national levels, and to be put into practice by local agencies at a local level. There are a number of reasons why this frequently proves difficult to do:

● the boundaries between education and training are poorly defined, and are becoming harder to distinguish as more and more education includes strong vocational elements, and as more and more training is delivered through educational techniques;
● in areas of highest unemployment there is often tension between national and local governments;

● national government policies are conceived in terms of the needs of cohorts of people — they are directed at statistics — whereas local policies are generally directed far more specifically at groups of people — they are directed more at individuals; individuals do not like to be treated as statistics;
● regardless of what people themselves like or dislike, national and local policies on the same issues tend often to have different objectives; on occasion, national measures are directed at short-term statistical improvements, whereas local use of them is in the context of medium or long-term improvements in individual prospects and circumstances; on other occasions national schemes directed at the improvement of serious education or training deficiencies or at job-creation, are taken up by local authorities simply because of the money involved.

The availability of economic information

One of the most common difficulties faced by agencies or groups of people concerned with starting new initiatives to train young people, and to develop new work opportunities for them is that of obtaining accurate local labour market information. This difficulty generally seems to be less serious when initiatives are the result of genuine cooperation between social partners locally, but even then the result can be that initiatives are provided with more information than they can make use of, and information which is uninterpreted. This is not necessarily the fault of the social partners, but is really just an indication of the changed circumstances of the labour market and the different techniques which must now be used to locate and make use of opportunities within it. When jobs were relatively plentiful, when training followed traditional lines, and when there was relative stability of employment, there was a low premium on gathering detailed labour market information. The opposite is true when jobs are scarce, when training in most Member States is undergoing substantial change and reform, and when labour market conditions are subject to considerable, and often violent change. Under these circumstances the labour market becomes an unfamiliar country, and the first priority is an accurate map. Time spent ensuring that such information is available, both for young people themselves, and also for those planning education, training and work creation initiatives for them, is never wasted.

The leading role

One of the consequences of achieving high levels of collaboration between social partners and a variety of local agencies and institutions can be an unwillingness of any single person or agency to assume leadership. Designing and developing services for young people is a difficult and high-risk activity. It is essential that it is assisted and protected by the consent of the individuals and the institutions, but it is also unlikely to succeed unless it is clear who is leading it. This may be an individual, or it may be an institution or an agency, but without leadership the effects of a high degree of coordination are more likely to be inertia than the vitality which is essential.

51

2.2.3. Coordinating resources and agencies

Institutional rivalry

A significant feature of developments in some Member States has been the proliferation of agencies and institutions at both local and national levels to deal with the problems which have been created by industrial and social change, and by the rise in unemployment amongst all age groups. These agencies and institutions have all performed useful tasks, but they also tend to find themselves in competition with each other for available resources — and sometimes even for the young people who are their clients.

There are other occasions where they find their basic values and priorities in conflict with each other. Those who come from educational roots may not share objectives with those who have developed their activities from social work roots or from vocational training roots. This can cause a great deal of conflict between agencies. This is very rarely to the advantage of the young unemployed.

The social partners

The single most important element in organizing the local coordination of services and resources for young people is securing the cooperation of local social partners. Without this it is impossible to guarantee that education, training, information and advice are consistent with labour market realities.

A further important consideration is that, while training innovations and temporary work schemes are invariably the result of social partner agreement at a national level, their successful implementation often depends on the active cooperation of social partners at a local level, where practical difficulties may emerge. Successful agreements at national level do not always guarantee that an initiative is fully acceptable and capable of being put into operation locally.

Relations with social partners are often made difficult by the fact that they are consulted once a scheme has been developed to the point of being implemented, and are not consulted at an early stage when their comments or reservations could be taken constructively into account. Consultation at the last moment often means that negative comments are seen as evidence of obstruction. It is greatly to the advantage of those who are developing initiatives to consult social partners as early as possible, and wherever feasible to include them in the design of what is proposed. It is also to the advantage of social partners to make the time to be involved as early as possible. It saves time wasted on disputes later on.

Small and medium-sized companies

In many localities major job growth is largely confined to expanding small and medium-sized enterprises. It is in these enterprises that the major opportunities lie for many young people. But small and medium-sized enterprises are often poorly represented by the social partners at national level, and at a local level frequently say that they are too busy to take an active role in educational, training and social matters. This can be a serious problem, resulting in the separation of education and training from the realities of the enterprises where most job growth is likely to take place. This is to the disadvantage of young people, whose links with this part of the labour market can be poor as a result. It is also to the disadvantage of the enterprises themselves which fail to keep providers of education and training fully informed of their current and future needs, and find themselves recruiting young people who have not been trained in the most effective manner.

Family and friends

What role do family and friends have to play in young people's transition to work and to adult life? The answer is less clear than it used to be when in many industries and occupations it was normal for young people to be introduced to employers by parents or by other family or local connections. This now happens much less than it did because of the great changes in the management, the size and the structure of enterprises in the face of economic and employment crises.

Both informally negotiated training opportunities and jobs themselves have become scarce in most sectors of activity (there are clear exceptions in the small and medium-sized enterprises in many Member States). At the same time there has been the widespread development of transition training by public agencies — formalizing what was once often an informal process. Advice and counselling are also now seen as expert services, which also have to be provided outside the context of family or friendship networks. It is always difficult to find a place for non-professional inputs to professional services, and yet it is quite clear that parents have a responsibility for overseeing the transition of their children into adult life; both parents and other relations and friends are frequently in a position to play important roles as guides or mentors. Initiatives which exclude the participation of such non-professionals are, because of that, less effective than they should be, but there seem to be no clear models available to show professionals how to integrate the assistance of parents and friends. This is an issue (amongst others) on which those responsible for measures which are largely concerned with training may usefully learn from their colleagues in the secondary schools. It is also an issue on which some practical research and development work might yield some important results.

Training of administrators and trainers

It is clear that changes in the ways in which programmes for young people are constructed and organized will require that many of those responsible receive some form of additional training. If they do not, they are likely to remain substantially within the confines of their own professionalism, and of the methods of their organizations, failing to make the adjustments necessary to cooperate with others.

The fact is that many administrators and trainers are beginning to find themselves dealing, for the first time in their lives, with multi-disciplinary programmes. Instead of working (as many of them may have done for most of their working lives) within the protection of single agencies, many are having to accommodate the quite different psychology and tactics of managing working relationships between quite different agencies and institutions. They are having to change their attitudes both to young people and to their own colleagues. They are having to accept both the relative narrowness of their own skills and experience, and also their own need to undertake demanding and difficult retraining. It is quite likely that in a great many cases the administrators and the trainers are subjected to at least as much stress as are the young people with whom they work. The nature and the extent of the training they need is only now beginning to be clarified. The techniques for providing it are being developed, but they have not been adequately incorporated into programmes, let alone made generally available. What is quite clear is that locally coordinated initiatives require to be served by local, multi-disciplinary staff-development facilities.

2.2.4. The special problems of non-industrial areas

National and international action programmes are invariably designed to be easily applicable in localities where need is quantitatively greatest. In the case of employment and training programmes this means that programmes designed for the European Community as a whole have been directed mostly at urban and industrialized areas of high population and high unemployment. They have also been focused largely upon needs in the north of Europe, and have been designed largely from the experience of experts from the north of Europe. In most Member States a similar pattern has prevailed. Programmes have been designed to respond to the needs of people living in areas where great industrial change has taken place, and attempts have then been made to apply the same programmes, with the same rules, the same financial provisions and the same approaches to learning in non-industrial and rural areas. This does not work.

Non-industrial and rural areas differ in many respects from urban and industrialized areas:

● They are often culturally very different, with different attitudes to work, and different expectations of income and career structure.

● In many rural areas there is, and has been for many decades, a problem of extensive out-migration of young people, leaving depopulated, ageing communities, lacking both skills and the motivation for change.

● Infrastructure which is commonplace in populated areas does not exist. Training initiatives and work-creation activities require premises and equipment. Premises frequently do not exist in rural areas. Equipment must be purchased specially.

● Transport is a problem because it is frequently not available and, when it is available, high cost because distances are often so great.

● In many areas there are housing shortages which affect young people's decisions to leave to seek work in urban and industrial centres or which result in problems for them if they stay.

It is important that the problems facing young people who live in non-industrialized and rural areas receive increased attention both at a Community level and at the level of Member States. There are three priorities:

(1) That new programmes should be developed which take special account of the needs of such young people, and of the education, training, employment and social potential of the localities in which they live.

(2) That the financing and administration of such programmes should reflect the special and administrative problems of these localities.

(3) That measures should be taken to adapt existing programmes developed on urban and industrial assumptions and guidelines to the different needs and circumstances of non-industrialized and rural areas.

Coordination and integration

A planned approach for administrators and practitioners at a local level

Contents

A planned approach

There is no way of achieving local coordination, or of arranging integration of services and facilities for young people, except through reasoned and careful planning. There are numerous approaches to planning educational and training programmes, and most of them are capable of being applied to the larger problems of integrating wide ranges of objectives and the services to respond to them.

Approaches and methods which are familiar and have been used successfully in the past are perfectly adequate for this task as well — as long as the right ingredients are inserted.

The purpose of this section is therefore to present a range of examples and models derived from the initiatives reflected in this handbook within the context of a planned approach. This is a convenient way of presenting the information so that it can be adapted into any other planning method, or used as it is.

This simply-organized planning approach is designed to satisfy two main criteria:

● It invites **all** ideas to be incorporated and stated at the start, and only filtered out as the process develops.

● It contains a strong element of evaluation, revision and replanning, not as some great and complex process which takes place at set intervals, but in the form of a series of critical but open questions posed at any time about each part and stage of the plan.

Planning and Replanning

Evaluating Revising Adapting

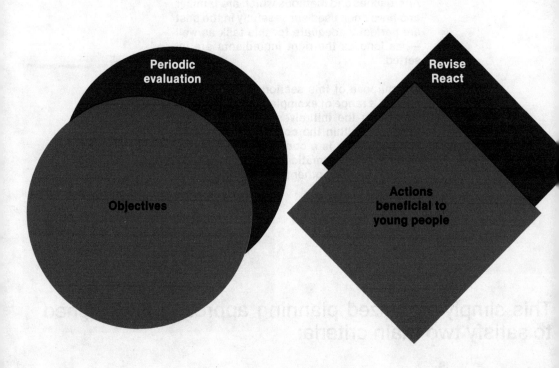

Periodic
evaluation

Objectives

Revise
React

Actions
beneficial to
young people

Forming plans

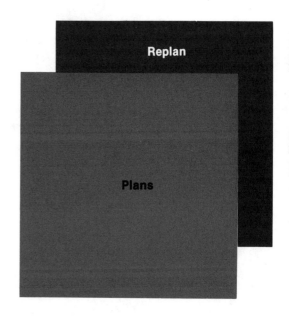

**Allow for change
of interests or views**

Limitations

Replan

Plans

page 103   **page 105**   page 106   **page 117**

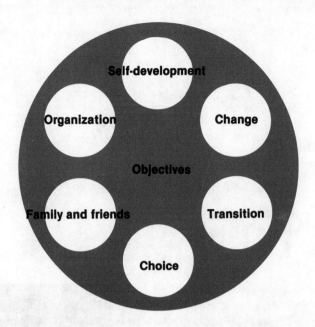

Objectives can only be formed in the light of understanding the processes through which young people are going as they make their transition from school to adult and working life.

To be effective, and fully embracing, objectives must cover these six processes:

Self-development

Providing every possible encouragement, assistance and resource to encourage young people to recognize and realize their own ambitions and abilities, and to test these against reality in education, training, work and social and personal life.

Change

Ensuring that the assumption that change will continue at a rapid rate, and that it may embrace all aspects of personal, family, social and working life, is built into all provision offered to young people. The objective is that they should be prepared to face change and to use it to their advantage rather than to be the victims of it.

Transition

Recognizing that the process of transition should be an organized and active one, which each young person controls for him or herself as far as possible. Rejecting the idea that young people should submit passively while an army of teachers, trainers, bureaucrats and social workers shift them from adolescence to adulthood.

Choice

Emphasizing that the widest range of options must be available to each young person. This is a basic tenet of equality of opportunity. It is also a pragmatic necessity when both work and the way in which life is lived are changing fast, and when relatively little is frequently known of young people's real abilities at the time when they finish compulsory education.

Family and friends

Including the social community of family, friends and local groups and organizations of all kinds as active resources, and even participants, in the transition of each young person.

Organization

Requiring that this vital stage in young people's lives (so much of it embodying learning and experimenting which can never be repeated) is effectively resourced and, where appropriate, organized. The most important part of this is the coordination of the complex range of services so that they are comprehensible and accessible to each young person.

An assessment of the nature of the operation of these processes in any particular locality leads to the formation of objectives.

They must answer the question, 'why make the effort, and incur the cost, of establishing methods of integrating services for young people?'

Objectives are then likely to be ranked roughly as follows:

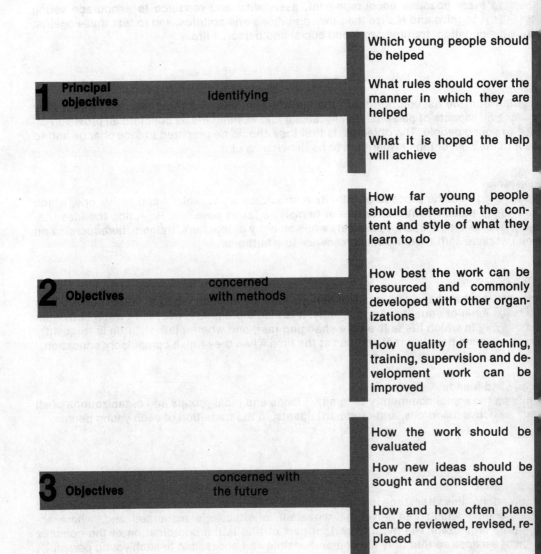

1 Principal objectives	identifying	Which young people should be helped
		What rules should cover the manner in which they are helped
		What it is hoped the help will achieve
2 Objectives	concerned with methods	How far young people should determine the content and style of what they learn to do
		How best the work can be resourced and commonly developed with other organizations
		How quality of teaching, training, supervision and development work can be improved
3 Objectives	concerned with the future	How the work should be evaluated
		How new ideas should be sought and considered
		How and how often plans can be reviewed, revised, replaced

Naturally, the written objectives of the initiatives contributing material to this handbook not fully coincide with these headings, or necessarily with the priority given to them. B they are derived from the same concerns, and from a shared general analysis.

Example

The broadest possible range of objectives is taken on by the *missions locales*. This concise description from *mission locale du pays de Lorient* illustrates the approach:

Objectives

To survey the situations and needs of young unemployed and unqualified people in the age group 16-26 in travel-to-work areas *(bassins d'emploi)*

To encourage local bodies in the development and provision of suitable answers

Functions

— receive, inform, and advise young people and monitor their progress;

— development of training programmes and introduction of young people to training;

— support of initiatives having as their objective the creation of jobs by and for young people;

— support of projects designed to develop the social qualifications of young people (health, accommodation, leisure activities, holidays, cultural activities);

— support of projects designed to develop the self-expression of young people.

Example **comtec**

A range of training, education and manpower objectives are articulated by the Irish Youth Employment Agency in its introduction to Comtec (Community training and employment consortia). These provide the basis for the activities of the Comtec set up in **Cork IRL.**

'In the new circumstances of high unemployment and less certainty about future needs, those education, training and employment services which are the responsibility of the agency must be judged against the extent to which:

● they ultimately make a net contribution to job-creation;

● they ensure that young people have the education and training needed to help them join the labour force and adapt to changing employment circumstances in the future;

● they provide a safety net which can locate and provide a second chance for those for whom the mainstream education and training structures have proved inadequate;

● they contribute to a coordinated approach to manpower problems in the country.'

Additional recognition is given to:

● the need for each Comtec to gain a thorough understanding of its labour force and market and their needs;

● the realignment of planning and management systems in major provider organizations to accommodate a more 'bottom up' participative approach;

● the establishment of planning and operational linkages with relevant providers outside the manpower services area which is the prime area of responsibility for Comtecs;

● the development of a system at national level for collating and reconciling local plans.

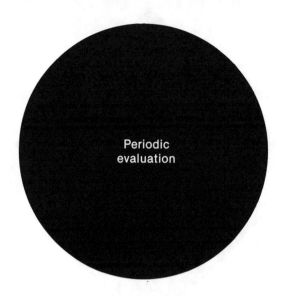

Periodic
evaluation

Periodic evaluation of objectives is essential based on:

1.
Is the target group still the same?

2.
**Is the approach to their problems
still relevant, and consistent with law?**

3.
Are the best professional methods either in use or in view?

Actions beneficial to young people

Schools should provide all young people with:

1 General education

Provided through the traditional academic and practical curriculum

by

Teachers
Parents

2 Knowledge and experience of the outside world

Acquired through work experience and community based activities

with

Employers
Voluntary agencies

3 Information and advice on training & further education, and employment opportunities

Passed on through individual and group counselling

by

Career services
Careers teachers
Employment agencies

There should be a follow-up system after school

Source: European Community transition II programme

Unfortunately this is still by no means always provided and if it is, may not be of a very high standard. (The pilot projects of the EC transition II programme provide examples of good practice in each Member State).

Any young person approaching a local initiative for help is liable to require a sequence of services and resources, beginning with high-quality information and advice. The level at which it starts will depend on the nature of local school-based provision, but it will always include:

What is on offer **must** include the widest possible access to vocational and educational opportunities — it will be greatly enhanced if it provides a means of relating personal and social services to the training and education — finally, it **must** provide an effective link with the job market.

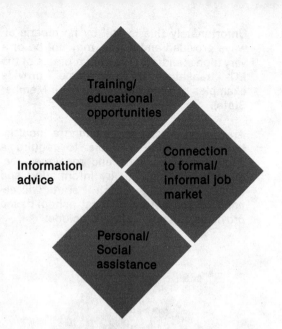

Training/
educational
opportunities

Information
advice

Connection
to formal/
informal job
market

Personal/
Social
assistance

Information and advice

In many respects this is the most important single component of any local provision.

If the range and quality of information and advice is comprehensive and good, then young people, educators and employers can have some confidence in the professional competence of the whole initiative. If it is of limited scope and of poor or variable quality, it will affect everything else which is attempted.

The ways in which information and advice are provided vary a great deal between Member States. A very complete illustration of a highly integrated system is provided in Denmark.

This illustration shows how the systematic provision of information and advice is built up in the last three years of secondary school — how the resources of a number of agencies and individuals are coordinated while young people attend vocational schools — and how a consistent link is maintained for two years after the end of secondary schooling:

Example

Danish law requires that in the two years after compulsory schooling has finished at 16 each young person's progress is followed by guidance counsellors based in the education system. Their job is to give each young person the help and advice he or she needs, and to do anything possible to help individuals or groups of young people to find training and work.

How guidance counsellors work:

'The job of guidance counsellors:

1. a.
To give counselling and guidance:

● when young people choose subjects at the vocational schools;

● in getting placement at the end of the first (EFG) year (the basic course) at vocational school;

● in helping with special needs;

● to students who want to drop out of courses by informing about other possibilities.

b.
Inform each student about his/her economic situation, tax questions, economic-student-support.

c.
Help solve personal problems and if necessary send the students to other experts.

d.
Give guidance to students who cannot get access to the education or training they wish.

e.
Help make schools more coordinated by:
● ensuring good introduction arrange-

ments for students at the beginning of each year;

● informing colleagues about the work of guidance counsellors;

● collaborating with school administrations and the teachers to guide individual students in connection with their choice of education/training.

2. a.
Establish and organize contact and collaboration between secondary schools, technical schools and commercial schools, local authorities, job-centres, labour and employer organizations, social security offices, etc.

b.
Help inform the outside world about the educational opportunities in technical and business schools.

c.
Get hold of appropriate guidance and counselling materials.

In fulfilling this task each guidance counsellor is under rules of professional secrecy, and the school administration cannot make a guidance counsellor act on behalf of a young person without his or her agreement.

Counsellors
1.
Have to be teachers and teach at least half time, and counselling is not to exceed 12 hours for business schools and 16 hours for technical schools (though this is often exceeded).

2.
A guidance counsellor gets 1 hour reduction from teaching per 10 students and takes care of between 100 and 160 students per year.'

Responsibility for helping young people make a smooth transition from school to work in Randers is carefully coordinated with responsibilities clearly defined:

Guidance counsellors	Job centres	Liaison committee of local social partners	Social Services Department
Personal counselling and guidance	Register students who have finished their one-year technical school or business school course	Organizes job-finding days	Takes special care of disadvantaged young people
Help with vocational choice and personal problems	Talk to students about job opportunities	Advertising campaigns	
Programmes of visits to employers		Mailing campaigns to employers	
		Sets up meetings with groups of employers	
Techniques for getting jobs		Arranges for employers and unions to brief young people about the labour market	
Job finding campaigns and schemes		Arranges classroom briefings	
Cooperation with public bodies and social partners			

Example

A quite different system, coordinating the resources of Sussex Training (West), the Chichester College of Technology and the local Careers Service *during* the period in which a young person is part of the Youth Training Scheme is illustrated below:

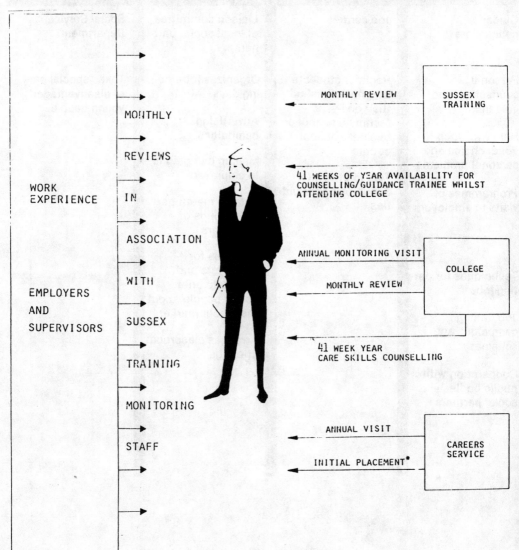

VERBUNDSYSTEM
Example **OBERHAUSEN**

Oberhausen has a regional advisory agency (RAA) specifically aimed at young migrants and the children of migrants. The RAA agency has a staff of five and a pool of 15 contract teachers who give six to eight hours a week of their time to working with young people at the end of their time at school and in the period before they find work.

They start their consulting process in the last three years of the secondary school and are able to talk to all the young foreign school-leavers in Oberhausen, between 750 and 800 each year. Besides this they organize supporting courses for young people with school problems and they have a very close connection to the various initiatives and institutions in the Oberhausen Verbundsystem.

Originally the main point of their work was to give advice to the young foreigners about the German school system and the different types of qualifications available. Now they deal more and more with the problems of the post-school period, focusing particularly on the very high percentage of young migrants who are unemployed.

They try to persuade employers and training establishments to accept a high ratio of young migrants on their qualification courses, in vocational training and in jobs.

The RAA, which stops working with individual young people at the point at which they find training places or work, is the only advisory facility for young migrants in Oberhausen, and is supported by a grant from the European Social Fund.

Example

mission locale
pour l'insertion sociale et professionnelle des jeunes

La Rochelle

How the *mission locale* advises and assesses each young person (this system is used for the 16-18 year-olds who come during the rush period between September and December each year). It involves four interviews in a period of 15 days.

The young person comes to the Mission locale

First encounter   received by a specialized person

— first interpretation of the demand
— meeting arranged with the person who seems to be most qualified within the multidisciplinary group

First discussion

— social worker
— guidance counsellor
— educator
— persons in charge of reception and training courses

Weekly meeting of the persons in charge of reception to study all the cases with the expert help of the guidance specialists and the vocational counsellor of ANPE in order to find the best solutions

collective information group:
information on opportunities

Second discussion with the same person

in order to decide together with the young person his/her guidance and choice taking into account the information he/she has received on the possibilities open to him/her

Data collection and storage in the computer as a preliminary step to follow-up

The team of the *mission locale* ensure the 'follow-up' of the decision by contacting the young person regularly (reminder from the computer)

- in order to enroll him/her in a course which corresponds to his/her wishes,
- in order to keep him/her updated on the results of the steps taken by the *mission locale,*
- in order to know the results of his/her personal approaches.

Example **·C··O·A··**

The COA reinforces the systems by which young people at school are advised about career choices by providing several hundred each year with the opportunity to taste a job for a week during school holidays in April and October.

These holiday courses, as they are called, are prepared in school by internal career counsellors on the basis of a workplan which they have constructed in collaboration with COA-Limburg.

These courses have been running for two years. In the second year COA-Limburg experimented with a follow-up to the holiday courses by giving the students the opportunity to talk about their plans for the future with career counsellors from career guidance offices.

The visits students pay to companies have to fit in with the whole process of career advice. For this reason a directory of opportunities is published about two months before the actual visit, so that the students can choose a place which corresponds with their preference.

In 1984 and 1985 about 1 500 young people have participated in these courses, receiving introduction to work in about 550 companies spread over Limburg.

Starting in August 1986 these orientation opportunities will be organized according to the scheme for work orientation, developed by COA-Rijnmond as a result of participating in the European Community's transition network animated by Ifaplan. This means structured preparation, work orientation and follow-up as a part of the educational programme in the participating schools.

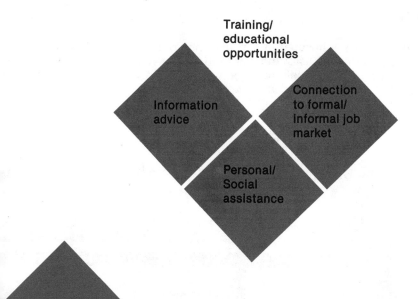

Training/
educational
opportunities

Information
advice

Connection
to formal/
informal job
market

Personal/
Social
assistance

Training and educational opportunities

The ways in which coordinating organizations influence the range and the quality of vocational and educational opportunities differ considerably. In some cases the influence they have is indirect, in others it is both direct and highly visible. Sometimes they work to persuade others to perform a task, or to make what they do more relevant to the needs of young people; on other occasions they act to fill an educational or training need themselves. The examples which follow are designed not so much to emphasize differences of organization, but rather to illustrate the range of what is already being stimulated, suggested or actually provided by some of the initiatives reflected in this handbook.

In particular, we provide examples of:

● a linked mixture of introductory training and vocational training,

● action to improve training for young women,

● innovatory training ideas,

● training of educators,

● new technology training.

VERBUNDSYSTEM

Example OBERHAUSEN

Within the Verbundsystem the member institutions provide a pattern of basic and vocational training according to their resources. Ruhrwerkstatt eV is a local community initiative. It provides a range of basic or introductory vocational training (Berufsvorbereitung) and also vocational training (Ausbildung).

Ruhrwerkstatt eV
District centre and
workshop

Akazienstr. 107
4200 Oberhausen 1
Tel. 80 17 36
80 38 24

Vocational training
Possible acquisition of school-leaving certificate
Personal development

AIM

Objective:
Certificate/
testimonial

Work sectors:
workshop — metalworking: basic skills and knowledge in the theory of metalworking occupations in the form of in-firm training (7 places)
workshop — construction: familiarization with various manual skills — self-developed projects and local help activities (8 places)
workshop — photo and video: basic knowledge of photography and video film production. Acquisition of schoolleaving certificate (8 to 9 places)
workshop — pottery: basic pottery skills through individual projects. Acquisition of school-leaving certificate (8 to 9 places)

Conditions for enrolment
Completion of compulsory schooling
Guidance by guidance service or job placement services of the employment office
Guidance provided by the local guidance office
Age: 16-25

Financial/material aids:
Pocket money DM 200 per month possibly public transport fares
Work clothing
Possibly grant under the vocational training promotion law

Working hours:
0815h- 1530h/1700 h

Programme begins:
At any time, as soon as a place is available

Duration:
6 months
to 1½ years

Vocational preparation

Training

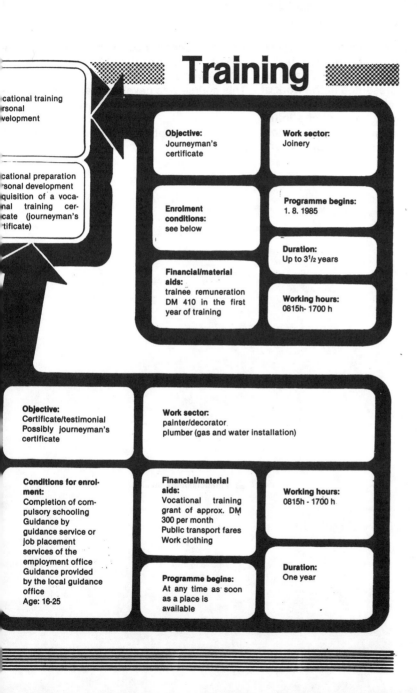

cational training
rsonal
velopment

cational preparation
rsonal development
quisition of a voca-
nal training cer-
cate (journeyman's
rtificate)

Objective:
Journeyman's
certificate

Work sector:
Joinery

**Enrolment
conditions:**
see below

Programme begins:
1. 8. 1985

Duration:
Up to 3 1/2 years

**Financial/material
aids:**
trainee remuneration
DM 410 in the first
year of training

Working hours:
0815h- 1700 h

Objective:
Certificate/testimonial
Possibly journeyman's
certificate

Work sector:
painter/decorator
plumber (gas and water installation)

**Conditions for enrol-
ment:**
Completion of com-
pulsory schooling
Guidance by
guidance service or
job placement
services of the
employment office
Guidance provided
by the local guidance
office
Age: 16-25

**Financial/material
aids:**
Vocational training
grant of approx. DM
300 per month
Public transport fares
Work clothing

Working hours:
0815h - 1700 h

Programme begins:
At any time as soon
as a place is
available

Duration:
One year

Example
La Rochelle

 mission locale
pour l'insertion sociale et professionnelle des jeunes

There are a number of initiatives designed to give direct help to young women. It is a strong objective of the *missions locales* as a whole, and well represented in the work of the *mission locale* at La Rochelle. Among the simplest and most basic of the initiatives is a short course of preparatory training designed to increase young women's confidence in themselves, to demystify the professional (and largely masculine) world, and to broaden their horizons. This course was developed and is administered by the *mission locale* itself.

The file description of this training project follows:

The La Rochelle *mission locale*

Scope:

Objective: **Guidance**

Date fixed for the start of activities: **1985**

To be concluded:

Action initiated by: *mission locale*

Action supported by: **Technical team of the *mission locale***

Role of the *mission locale* in this scheme: **Initiation, follow-up**

Partners: **Training organizations — Delegation for Women's Rights**
Member of Parliament Madame Colette Chaignaud

Objectives of this scheme:

Try to make it possible for young women who come for guidance or help in finding employment to get access to large workshops and to machines which are usually operated by men, so as to:

. enable women to get confidence in themselves,
. demystify the operations and executive positions which are traditionally considered to be masculine,
. enlarge the field of possible employment for women.

Approach:　— trainers,
　　　　　— training establishments, so that this scheme is completely integrated in teaching projects and well understood by those in charge of the workshops where these new target groups will be received.

Expected results of this scheme:**To be awaited**

Principal difficulties encountered:

Convince the training organizations of the usefulness of this scheme.
Try to get the trainers and the young people to view this scheme as part of an integral whole with respect to guidance, on a more or less long-term basis (guidance or entry).
Make it a systematic scheme.

Example

The *mission locale* du pays de Lorient, has
set up a centre for training young people in
the design and manufacture of neon lighting. It is the only centre of its kind in France,
and is an example both of the potential for
innovative training approaches and also of
the benefits of a level of national coordination between the 100 French *missions
locales.*

The group of between 20 and 30 trainees is
drawn from amongst local young people,
where there is a demand for training, and
also from any other parts of France where
young people can benefit from the training.
A proportion of the trainees are from
outside the Lorient area, and they are also
provided with accommodation.

The qualifications obtained are fully acceptable elsewhere in France, and are approved by the Federation de l'Enseigne Lu-
mineuse, the regulating body for training in
neon lighting. As well as the *mission locale*
and this regulatory body, educational and
training interests and the Mairie of Inzinzac,
where the centre has been set up, are involved with the support and further development of the centre.

Example

mission locale
pour l'insertion sociale et professionnelle des jeunes

La Rochelle

The *mission locale* at La Rochelle has joined with its equivalent at Pau in Aquitaine to set up a training course in cuisine which recognizes the demands of seasonal labour. Called 'Mer-Montagne', it trains young people, and gives them work experience at La Rochelle in the summer tourist season, and in the Pyrenees during the winter skiing season.

The alternate training provided in the scheme breaks down into:

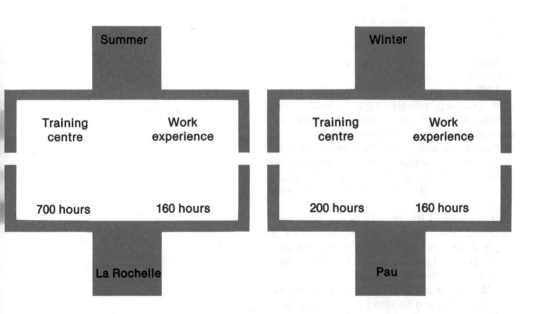

The scheme is designed initially for 16 trainees: 8 each from La Rochelle and Pau.

The design and the terms and conditions of this course are agreed by AMOF (Association main d'œuvre formation), which exists to protect the circumstances of unskilled, seasonal and highly mobile workers.

Example ··C·O·A··

An important part of COA Limburg's task is to design projects on a Province-wide basis. One has been concerned with ensuring that young people are well prepared at school for the demands which information technology will make on them in the workplace. A large part of this preparation is delivered by teachers, so it is absolutely necessary that these teachers' knowledge is completely up to date.

Because of the current lack of understanding of information technology within schools COA Limburg has, in participation with other institutions in the area, developed a plan for training teachers.

This plan is connected to a national scheme of training development of educational software and introduction of microcomputers to schools.

In 1985 a small pilot project was set up by COA Limburg, consisting of two-day sensibility courses and one-week work experience periods in companies.

The objective was to give teachers a chance to renew their knowledge by practical experience and to give them an adequate basis on which to choose additional training.

On the basis of the results of the pilot project and other corresponding activities a larger plan with the same objective has been set up in Limburg by COA Limburg and other organizations.

The idea behind the national plan, of which this COA Limburg scheme is a part, is that three teachers in each school will be trained, and they will then deliver the training to the rest of their colleagues. In Limburg this means that the COA has planned to provide courses for around 2 000 teachers. The courses are timed to take place just after hardware and software has been delivered to the schools.

In addition some 200 vocational and general education teachers will have the chance of one month of practical work experience, during which time they will be replaced in their schools. The project lasts for two and a half years from August 1986, and its products will be available for application in other parts of the Netherlands.

Example

It has been estimated that there will be a need between 1985 and 1989 for about 15 000 young people in Holland trained in the new information technologies. A national study on the needs of companies has resulted in three ministries putting together a programme for training of programmers (targeted at high-level general education) and for microcomputer assistants (for trainees at a lower level).

The scheme was designed on the assumption that it would be organized at a local level by competent managing agencies.

In Limburg there were some doubts about the labour market relevance of the project, so COA Limburg was asked to investigate the needs of the Limburg labour market in relation to the objectives of the new training programme. At the same time COA Limburg prepared the start of the project, using the results of the inventory.

This preparation meant:

1.
Investigating qualified available training facilities in existing schools and training centres;

2.
Arranging opportunities for work experience on a basis of young people spending five months in school (off-the-job) and five months in companies (on-the-job training);

3.
Identifying the conditions necessary to making the programme effective, such as specification of target group, acceptance and cooperation on a wide scale, financial possibilities, contents of the programme, connection to other training possibilities, organization, etc.

4.
Coordinating and stimulating participation of existing agencies in (parts of) the project.

COA Limburg concluded that, if the project was carried out according to the guidelines as put in the final handbook, it would improve young people's chances on the labour market.

The project started in Limburg in February 1986 with about 65 students and will be built up over a three-year period.

The responsibility for managing the project lies with a regional agency, run in partnership by trade unions and employers' organizations.

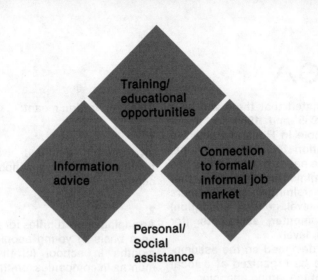

Training/
educational
opportunities

Information
advice

Connection
to formal/
informal job
market

Personal/
Social
assistance

Personal and social assistance

All the initiatives represented in this handbook would undoubtedly confirm that they are actively concerned for the personal and social welfare of the young people with whom they work. There are two degrees of concern, however:

● the readiness to assist or to find assistance for young people who have particular problems;

● the inclusion of specific activities directed at the solution of personal and social problems within the programmes of the initiative.

All responsible managers of initiatives for young people can demonstrate their ability to respond to young people's difficulties effectively. It is much less usual to find wider social education and activities integrated with vocational education and training.

Only two of the initiatives are formally in that position.

VERBUNDSYSTEM
Example OBERHAUSEN

The Verbundsystem itself was developed from within, created by awareness on the part of activists living and working in deprived parts of Oberhausen of the physical needs of the locality, and the social and vocational needs of its inhabitants. Within the Verbundsystem, Ruhrwerkstatt provides both training and education, and also a wide range of social and personal advice. It also refers young people to more specialist centres of advice within Oberhausen, among them the RAA for young immigrants (see previous example).

Example   **mission locale**
pour l'insertion sociale et professionnelle des jeunes

All 100 French *missions locales* are charged with providing personal and social solutions for young people, at the same time as they seek vocational solutions. Their philosophy is based on the contention that success in vocational education or training is likely to be closely linked to satisfactory:

health,

housing,

leisure,

family and social life.

An example of how these concerns are followed up is the work of the *mission locale* in La Rochelle in promoting improved health amongst the young people they work with. A relatively high incidence of health problems was noticed among the young people.

Now **each** young person coming to the *mission locale* is interviewed about his or her health and an assessment made of any immediate needs (dental care for instance). These needs are met by immediate referral to an appropriate doctor. At the same time efforts are made, through education, to persuade young people away from smoking, drugs and excessive drinking. The *mission locale's* work is based upon the belief that many young people are seriously handicapped in their working lives through poor health, lack of health care, and ignorance of the real effects of damaging habits. However well-motivated they may be, they are unlikely to succeed fully either in training or in work if their health is poor.

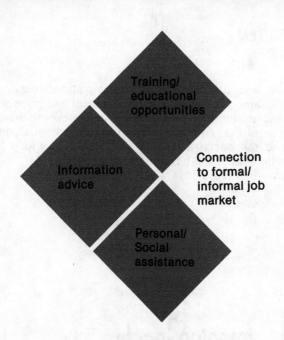

Training/
educational
opportunities

Connection
to formal/
informal job
market

Information
advice

Personal/
Social
assistance

Advocacy on behalf of young people

Wherever there are more young people than available jobs it is both reasonable and logical that extra efforts should be made to represent their skills effectively to employers:

Example

Each year there is an 'initiative day' in Randers. This is the focal point of the year's efforts in providing information, advice, access to educational and training opportuni-ties, and a route to work for young people in the two years after they have left the compulsory school system.

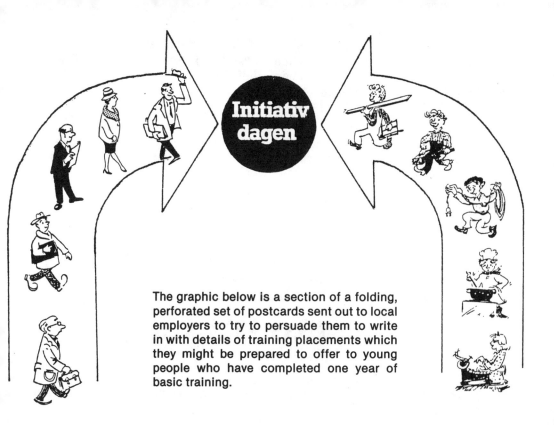

The graphic below is a section of a folding, perforated set of postcards sent out to local employers to try to persuade them to write in with details of training placements which they might be prepared to offer to young people who have completed one year of basic training.

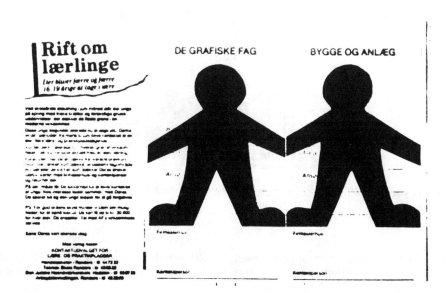

An extract from a further piece of material directed at employers reminds them that the cohort of 17 year-olds in the population reached a peak in 1984, and will fall rapidly (except for a slight climb between 1978 and 1980, and another in 1993) until the end of the century.

The success of the whole approach depends upon three things:

- the professionalism (including the very important production of interesting and attractive graphics) of the staff of the initiative;

- the motivation of the young people;

- the close involvement of their parents, who can also act as advocates for their own children.

There are going to be fewer and fewer young people

Der bliver færre og færre unge.

Believe it or not . . . but already from next year the number of 17 year-olds will fall. We will in future years be speaking about a direct shortage of young people for places as apprentices and trainees.

Number of 17 year-olds   1974 — 2 000

Der bliver hurtigt mangel på elever!

There is soon going to be a shortage of trainees.

That is why you should find your future younger staff members — now. In one year it might be too late.

The approach is extended throughout each year with a variety of activity and open days, mail shots to employers, direct contact with employers, and a strong emphasis on the young people themselves taking an active role.

Example

Sussex Training (West)

Trainees placed by Sussex Training with local employers are visited regularly by staff whose job it is to monitor their progress, and also to check with the employer whether or not there remains a good chance of a subsequent job. If there is not, then the trainee will, in most circumstances, be moved to an employer offering a real opportunity of permanent employment. In this way training is matched more closely to job vacancies, and young people know that their job prospects are receiving constant attention.

Job creation

What is the point of training young people to work, and then failing to provide them with jobs?

Training, particularly when its educational content is high, can be justified for its own sake in many circumstances when jobs — though not immediately available — may be in prospect. It is much harder, however, to answer the question when young people are being trained in localities where there are no apparent prospects of work in the short or the medium-term.

In these localities — and they exist in almost every Member State — the question itself is wrong. Instead of asking why it is worth training young people to work when there are no jobs, one should ask, 'Why continue to train young people for conventional jobs and as employees, when it would be better to train them for less conventional jobs, and to employ themselves by starting their own small enterprises?'

This kind of training is being developed, and it is inevitable that interest will grow in it for at least as long as the employment prospects of many young people recede.

It is also inevitable that the innovative approaches to this will be developed by those agencies which are strongly identified with particular localities, by those which are dedicated to a range of aims, and by those which are outside public institutional structures.

The following example from the Oberhausen Verbundsystem illustrates all these points.

VERBUNDSYSTEM
Example OBERHAUSEN

Three projects with different aims providing combined vocational training and job creation for young people.
Three projects within the Verbundsystem are working cooperatively to explore and develop different approaches to **creating** jobs for young people combined with their vocational training. In each case the projects have expanded their objectives to include work creation as it has become more difficult for young people — even with training — to find work.

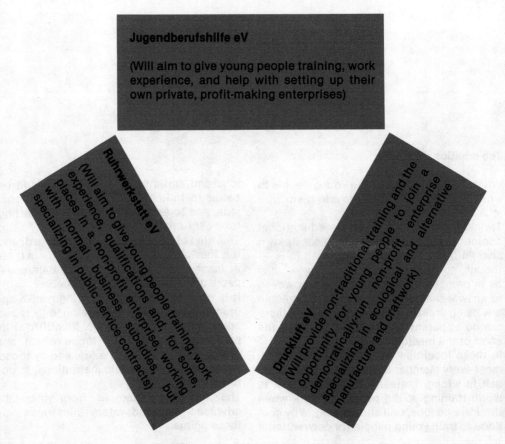

Jugendberufshilfe eV

(Will aim to give young people training, work experience, and help with setting up their own private, profit-making enterprises)

Ruhrwerkstatt eV

(Will aim to give young people training, work experience, qualifications and, for some, places in a non-profit enterprise, working with normal business subsidies, but specializing in public service contracts)

Druckluft eV

(Will provide non-traditional training and the opportunity for young people to join a democratically-run non-profit enterprise specializing in ecological and alternative manufacture and craftwork)

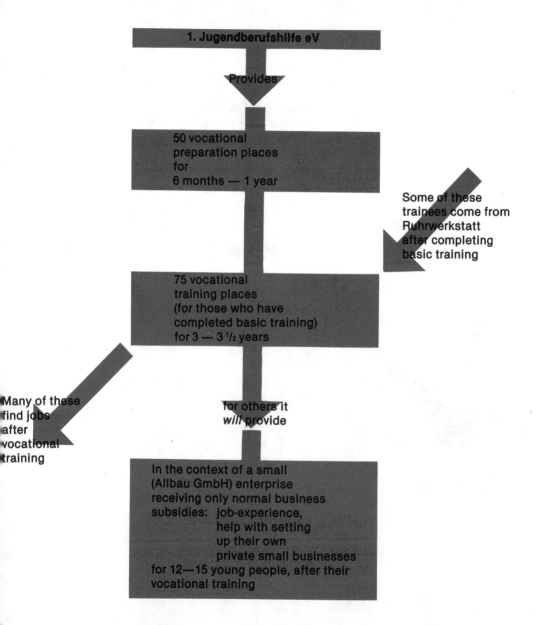

1. Jugendberufshilfe eV

Provides

50 vocational
preparation places
for
6 months — 1 year

Some of these
trainees come from
Ruhrwerkstatt
after completing
basic training

75 vocational
training places
(for those who have
completed basic training)
for 3 — 3 ½ years

Many of these
find jobs
after
vocational
training

For others it
will provide

In the context of a small
(Allbau GmbH) enterprise
receiving only normal business
subsidies: job-experience,
                help with setting
                up their own
                private small businesses
for 12—15 young people, after their
vocational training

This centre provides a range of training which leads young people towards conventional employment. But in spite of good relations with employers, this has become increasingly difficult. As a result an enterprise has been set up to provide employment for qualified young people who have no other employment prospects. It will operate fully within the labour market, and will develop activities in gardening, joinery, metalwork and building.

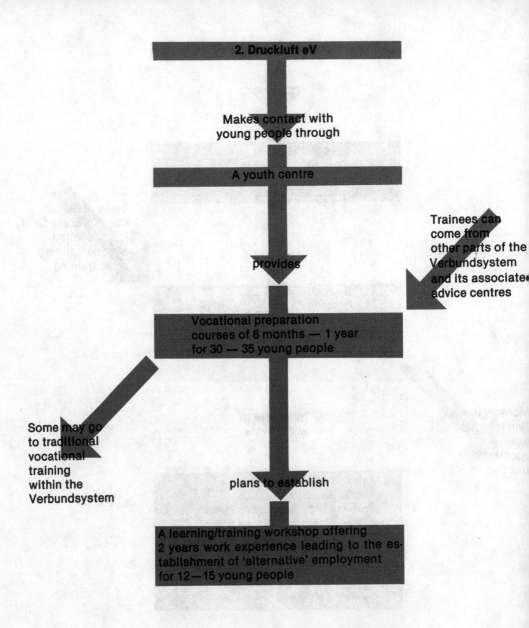

2. Druckluft eV

Makes contact with
young people through

A youth centre

provides

Trainees can
come from
other parts of the
Verbundsystem
and its associated
advice centres

Vocational preparation
courses of 6 months — 1 year
for 30 — 35 young people

Some may go
to traditional
vocational
training
within the
Verbundsystem

plans to establish

A learning/training workshop offering
2 years work experience leading to the establishment of 'alternative' employment
for 12—15 young people

Druckluft eV was founded by a group of young people who intended to try to create new alternative products and services. The enterprise will only be for young people who want to work in a 'cooperative' way, and who therefore can demonstrate strong personal commitment. They will specialize in ecological and improvement work, and will look for market 'niches' for which they can engage in small-scale manufacturing.

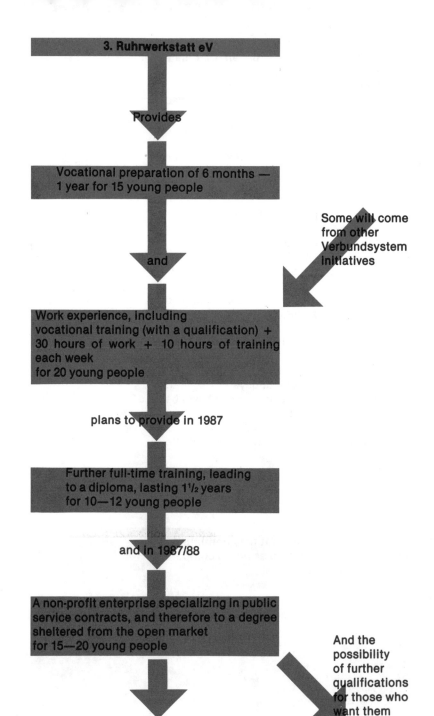

3. Ruhrwerkstatt eV

Provides

Vocational preparation of 6 months — 1 year for 15 young people

Some will come from other Verbundsystem initiatives

and

Work experience, including vocational training (with a qualification) + 30 hours of work + 10 hours of training each week for 20 young people

plans to provide in 1987

Further full-time training, leading to a diploma, lasting 1½ years for 10—12 young people

and in 1987/88

A non-profit enterprise specializing in public service contracts, and therefore to a degree sheltered from the open market for 15—20 young people

And the possibility of further qualifications for those who want them

This approach, within the local centre's programmes of work on behalf of disadvantaged (marginalized) young people, acknowledges the growing difficulty of finding jobs for young people who have received some training, unless they are able and willing to enter the traditional vocational training system. It is not considered realistic to attempt to set up business activities on the open labour market, so an enterprise which will seek public service work is being set up. The enterprise is expected to specialize in environmental work and in housing and repair activities, many of them in collaboration with other initiatives within the Verbundsystem. Early work will depend heavily on public subventions, but it is planned to rely less on these as the enterprise becomes better established, and the workers more experienced.

It is important to note that:

● These are the only work-creation projects planned within the Verbundsystem so that all available assistance and goodwill will be concentrated of them.

● They will cooperate with the private sector.

● They will do labour-only costed work for each other.

● They will all ensure that they continue to develop different work so as not to compete in any way with each other.

Revise
React

Every agency and **every piece of work** need to be reassessed regularly. Are they still as **well-targeted,** as **efficient,** as **effective** and as **innovative** as they were?

If not they must be **revised.**

Innovators must show that they too can **continue to react** to change. Otherwise they will themselves become outdated.

All the examples used to illustrate ideas in this handbook have been developed in response to the inability of previously existing institutions to change, or to the fact that no relevant institutions existed.

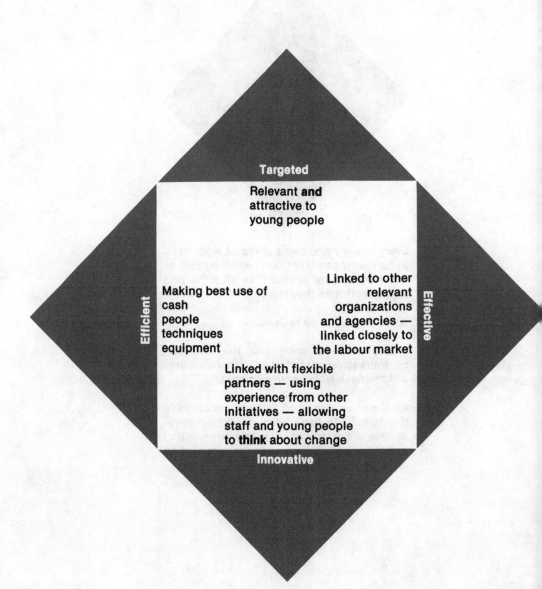

Targeted

Relevant **and**
attractive to
young people

Efficient

Making best use of
cash
people
techniques
equipment

Linked to other
relevant
organizations
and agencies —
linked closely to
the labour market

Effective

Linked with flexible
partners — using
experience from other
initiatives — allowing
staff and young people
to **think** about change

Innovative

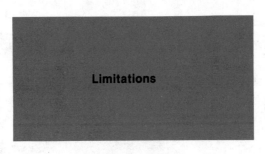

Limitations

All good ideas have to be tested against reality. This is not negative — it is just commonsense.

It is essential when ideas are being examined which have been developed in other countries, or in different political, economic and social systems, that they are looked at in the light of a number of possible limitations. Some of these may force abandonment of a project — others may prompt its revision — others may just require some small changes or realignments.

A feasible plan must satisfy clear criteria in relation to . . .

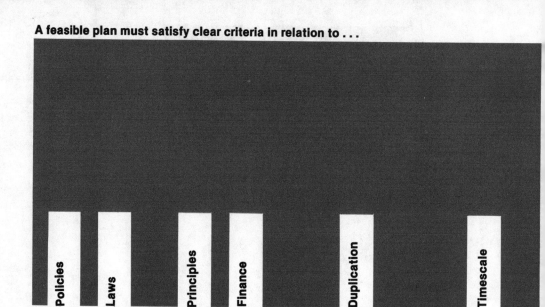

Policies **Laws** **Principles** **Finance** **Duplication** **Timescale**

They may be out of date and due for change. It may be right to try to change them. Someone else may be working to do that.

There is only a limited amount of negotiation to be done. Principles cannot be compromised too far. Finance can be negotiated, but unless a sufficient amount is available work cannot begin.

Everyone concerned with innovation and coordination is told that they are duplicating. Sometimes it is true, usually it is just natural reaction or jealousy.

Must be consistent with meeting the objectives.

Reassessment and revision of plans is usually necessary to some degree. It takes account of reality, and it often gives time for overall improvements. In many cases it will translate a good idea into a **viable project** . . .

but

All planning is a matter of compromise, adjustment of ideals to fit with realities. But in the end, if the essential principles behind a project cannot be preserved, or if some outside force resists it on grounds of law or policy, or if the money is not available, or if the job cannot be done in the time, it must be **postponed or abandoned** .

Allow for change of interests or views

One thing is certain . . . . that all these factors are subject to change, sometimes with great speed.

This has frequently proved to be the case with initiatives proposed for young people. When first devised, the initiators have been told that they are unnecessary, too expensive, merely duplicating the efforts of other people. Within months rather than years (usually prompted both by further worsening of unemployment, and by changes of attitude to new ideas), they become essential, a good investment, and a necessary means of coordinating resources.

Anyone who sets out to work with new ideas must expect to meet frustrations of this kind, and must be ready, when circumstances or official opinions change, to re-examine these seven criteria, and to be prepared to implement what previously seemed impossible.

It may also happen that a project which was previously viable becomes impossible to sustain. If this is so, it is vital to recognize the fact quickly, and act upon it.

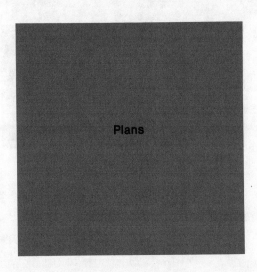

Plans

There is no blueprint for a local approach to providing young people with vocational education, training and the personal and social services they need to transfer effectively to working life. There is certainly no single way of designing and illustrating an interdependent system. The striking thing about the two illustrations which follow is that they are so similar, although they are represented in ways pictorially which reflect the differences of approach between France and the Federal Republic of Germany. They both do what is most important — they provide a kind of map, intelligible to young people as well as professionals and to politicians and administrators which indicates something of how an integrated system works, and which also indicates clearly how an individual young person might move through the system.

VERBUNDSYSTEM
Example OBERHAUSEN

In the Oberhausen Verbundsystem the centre is taken up by the pivotal function of advice and counselling from which young people move to vocational preparation, skill training and work. The illustration also shows the relationship of the social partners, the schools, other advice services, and of teachers, trainers and young people themselves to the Verbundsystem.

Network: 'Transition from school to working life'

Working group — youth unemployment — providers
- Chambers of Industry and Commerce/Craft Chambers
- Schools
- Youth guidance/counselling offices
- German Trades Union Federation
- Labour authorities
- Independent providers

Coordination service

Working group — youth unemployment — professional groups — plant management — trainers/instructors — social workers — teachers

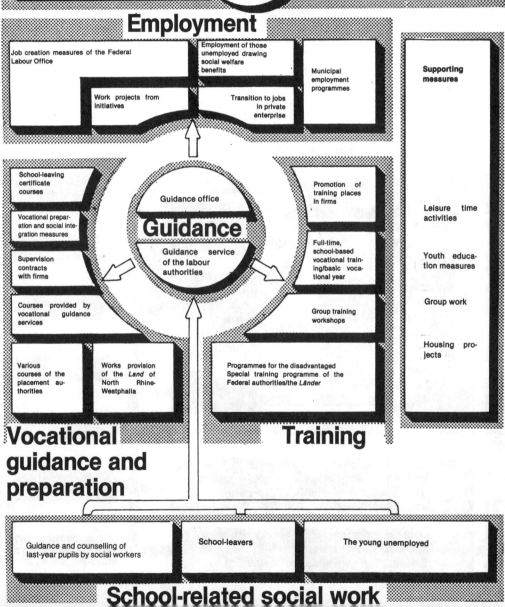

Employment

Job creation measures of the Federal Labour Office

Employment of those unemployed drawing social welfare benefits

Municipal employment programmes

Work projects from initiatives

Transition to jobs in private enterprise

Guidance

Guidance office

Guidance service of the labour authorities

School-leaving certificate courses

Vocational preparation and social integration measures

Supervision contracts with firms

Courses provided by vocational guidance services

Various courses of the placement authorities

Works provision of the *Land* of North Rhine-Westphalia

Promotion of training places in firms

Full-time, school-based vocational training/basic vocational year

Group training workshops

Programmes for the disadvantaged Special training programme of the Federal authorities/the *Länder*

Supporting messures

Leisure time activities

Youth education measures

Group work

Housing projects

Vocational guidance and preparation

Training

Guidance and counselling of last-year pupils by social workers

School-leavers

The young unemployed

School-related social work

Example

100 missions locales pour l'insertion des jeunes

The illustration of the progression available to a young person aged 16-18 which reflects reality for the *Missions locales* in Lorient and La Rochelle applies equally to the other 98 in areas of high unemployment throughout the country. They are coordinating and helping adapt to local use, and to the needs of young people, a complex but flexible system of opportunities.

Age group 16—18
A qualification through alternance training

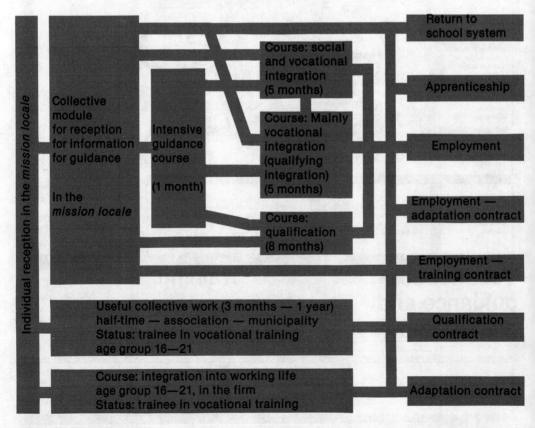

Example **comtec**

The brief for the Comtec (Community training and employment consortia) sets out the range of information considered necessary to forming a view of integrated education, training and manpower needs.

Each Comtec will be required to proceed through and document the following stages:

a. A collation of data on:

● school-leaving patterns and the destinations of school-leavers;

● unemployment (youth and adult) — distribution and special characteristics;

● existing manpower services provision and plans by each provider;

● school-based education and training provision (full and part-time);

● the extent of local assessment, counselling and guidance services and their distribution (whether manpower or educationally-based);

● the identifiable needs of the local labour market and the matching of local training provision to it;

● the scale and source of funding by programme, for youth employment and training services in the area.

b. The identification of:

● disadvantaged groups and areas within the locality;

● gaps in the linkage between schools and the manpower services;

● under/over provision for particular categories of young people, types of jobs or locations.

c. An assessment of:

● the appropriateness of scale and nature of current provision for the area;

● the extent of the actual and potential involvement of individual community-managed projects;

● the barriers to the development of such community management;

● the need for additional provision whether nationally or locally delivered.

d. The formulation of a two-year plan for approval by the Youth Employment Agency, based on the findings of the earlier stages including the establishment of an information process at local level to monitor its implementation.

The illustrations from the initiatives linked with this handbook, and the longer descriptions of their activities in Part Five, provide a wide range of examples of varied objectives, structures and methods. In particular, they may be of use in planning new initiatives for their illustration of:

A local social and community base	Verbundsystem Oberhausen
A national support and funding structure	Missions locales Lorient and La Rochelle
Planning relationship mixing educational and training effort and resources	Comtec Cork
Developed planning role, with devolution to local centres	COA Limburg
Working relationships with local employers, especially small and medium-sized enterprises (SMEs)	Sussex Training (West)
A strong information and advice structure	Business School/ Technical School Randers

Close examination of the initiatives also reveals a range of **criteria** which may usefully be applied to the planning of new initiatives aimed at providing an integrated and co-ordinated range of services and resources for young people.

A checklist of criteria for local coordinated initiatives

Criteria	Important and key elements

Location

A local base — one that is identifiable as a community, an employment catchment area, or a local administrative unit

Clear objectives linking national policies with local interests

Large enough to include a full range of local institutions — not so large as to be a region rather than a locality. (A number of the initiatives connected with this handbook serve localities of 120 000 — 150 000 inhabitants)

Agreement of the need for new structures, and for new ways of making use of existing facilities

Commitment to support a properly planned and evaluated initiative, which has an assured period (a minimum of 2 years) to establish itself

Young people

Contact and working relationships with social agencies and informal groups which serve young people, or which have contact with them

Participation by young people, where practical, in policy and management

Self-management
Cultural activities
Leisure
Housing
Personal and family matters
Drugs
Alcohol
Health
Finance

Local support

Formal and informal relationships with social partners and local political and social organizations

Representative management comittees
Fresh ideas

Criteria	Important and key elements

National support

Professional links to national education and training agencies for information, support of staff and joint action to change national policies and facilities

Staff training
Training materials
Fresh ideas

Local operations

A high quality information and advice system available to all young people, offering access to all information sources relevant to young people's lives, not just to employment, training and educational information and advice

Basic training
Vocational education
New technology education and training (demystification)
Vocational training
Innovatory training
On and off-the-job training and work experience

Access to educational and training courses in partnership with local 'institutions' and agencies — and an ability to change those courses and help design new and better ones

Temporary work
Job and enterprise creation

Training for trainers, teachers, staff of initiatives

Close relationship with local employers and unions — acceptance as a part of the structure of the labour market

Resources

Mixed national and local funding

Ability to make flexible use of public and private sector support in money and in kind

Planning
Studies
Contact with young people
Linking agencies and institutions
Designing programmes
Training trainers and staff
Carrying out training
(where appropriate)

Initiatives in non-industrial and rural areas depend for their success on a number of vitally important additional criteria

Unless these are first acknowledged, and then thought through in the context of both national and European Community programmes, rural and non-industrial areas in the northern Member States will share with large parts of southern and Mediterranean Member States systems for transitional education and training which place their young people at a clear disadvantage.

These criteria are designed to show how equality of opportunity can be improved, and also to contribute to the development of circumstances in which trained people — the essential prerequisite of job creation — can begin to construct a wider and more varied employment base.

Criteria	Important and key elements

Location

Catchment areas for coordinated initiatives must coincide as far as possible with recognized labour markets or communities with broadly consistent economic and social interests. This may often mean that a viable area for coordination contains no more than a quarter or half the number of people in a comparable urban area.

Separate planning criteria for non-industrial and rural initiatives

Finance

All financial arrangements must acknowledge the greater cost per head of organizing initiatives in non-industrial areas, and particularly in isolated rural areas. If young people living in them are to experience equality of treatment with young people living in urban areas, there must be special financial provisions.

Special financial provisions are needed for:

transport (costs are *always* greater);

educational and training equipment (it is often necessary to make up for past underinvestment compared to urban and industrial areas, and it must also be accepted that higher capital allowances per head are often needed in order to ensure that individual young people get reasonable access to equipment);

Criteria	Important and key elements

Finance

housing and lodging
(adequate housing for young people in rural
areas frequently does not exist, and there is
need in some localities to arrange for them
to be lodged away from their homes if they
are to take full advantage of educational or
training programmes).

Content and structure of education and training

Recognition of the fact that participation by industry in training may be difficult or impossible if young people are to be trained in non-industrialized and rural areas. Larger companies do not exist. Small and medium-sized enterprises generally have neither the resources, nor the background expertise or interest to make contributions along conventional lines.

Encouragement for non-conventional training schemes.

Special priority for introducing new information technology to rural areas.

There must be special attention paid to prospects for agriculture-related work, for job and enterprise creation, and to the role of new information technologies in bringing new work into rural communities.

Development of mixed and multi-skill training programmes to prepare for part-time and mixed occupations.

There must be provisions to ensure that teachers and trainers working in rural areas are themselves properly trained for their work. They find themselves working within different and older traditions than those which apply in industrial areas. Often there is resistance to change. There is usually a healthy resistance to fashion.

Special teacher and trainer development courses, based on shared experience from other non-industrial and rural areas.

Special priority given to the design of appropriate courses for girls, and to the best and most flexible ways of providing them in isolated localities.

There must be some allowances and compensation for the fact that groups of young people who have difficulty in getting fair and equal access to training and jobs in urban and industrialized areas, are likely to be in even more difficulty in non-industrial and rural areas, where resources are fewer,

| Criteria | Important and key elements |

Content and structure of education and training

where cultural prejudices may still exist, and where their own expectations may be very low.

Culture

Non-industrial and rural areas are not smaller versions of urban and industrial areas. They are culturally different, and they must be seen as a source of richness and variety of opportunity, not as a problem. It must be acknowledged and encouraged.

Taking these factors into account, a plan should result in an initiative set in a clear relation-ship to local and national institutions and phenomena, and involving itself in a wide range of activities.

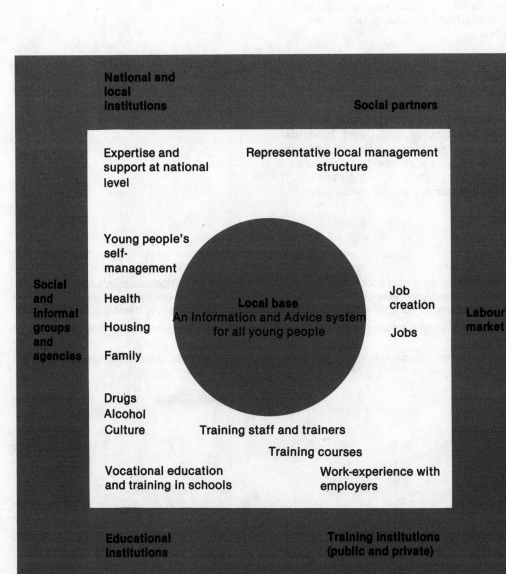

National and
local
institutions

Social partners

Expertise and
support at national
level

Representative local management
structure

Social
and
informal
groups
and
agencies

Young people's
self-
management

Health

Housing

Family

Local base
An Information and Advice system
for all young people

Job
creation

Jobs

Labour
market

Drugs
Alcohol
Culture

Training staff and trainers

Training courses

Vocational education
and training in schools

Work-experience with
employers

Educational
institutions

Training institutions
(public and private)

n constantly changing circumstances, every plan must be subject to revision as a result of new ideas, evaluation, changed needs of young people, and altered economic and social circumstances.

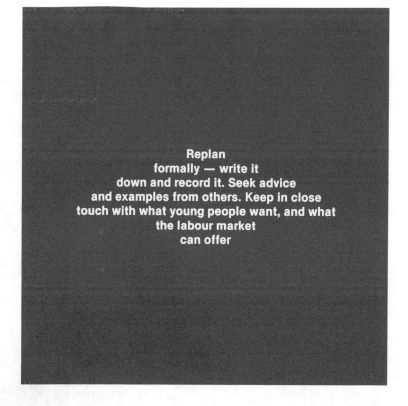

Replan
formally — write it
down and record it. Seek advice
and examples from others. Keep in close
touch with what young people want, and what
the labour market
can offer

National and Community policies, mechanisms, guidelines, policy framework and proposals

Contents

4.1.1. The whole purpose of this handbook is to illuminate and to reinforce the initiatives which have been taken in various Member States to provide local means of giving young people a better ordered and assisted transition from school into working and adult life. In this it rests largely upon the examples of different approaches to this, which are distinct from each other in their origins, and in numerous ways in their methods. The differences between them are clear enough, but the important thing is that they are similar in a number of basic and vital respects, and these similarities are themselves of great significance for the development of future policies on transition. Among the most important similarities are:

a.

The fact that each of the initiatives strongly represents the analysis that, whatever is permitted or demanded at a Community or at a national level, the responsibility for ensuring that young people can make an effective transition from school and childhood to adult and working life must be **locally** discharged as far as possible, and will be discharged better if what is done contains a considerable element of locally inspired design. This reflects the acceptance that local labour markets differ substantially one from another, that they always have done, and that they are likely to differ even more from each other in a period when much job growth is confined to new and to small and medium-sized enterprises, than they have done in the past when large employers and public authorities accounted for so many new jobs. It reflects the understanding that education, training and other services for young people are likely to be of better quality and relevance if the people who deliver them from day to day feel that they have the ability to tailor what they do to local needs and opportunities. It reflects the growing acceptance throughout the education system, and amongst policymakers that the social partners have an important role in providing both advice and direct assistance to make education and training better preparations for the realities of the workplace. This can be done to a degree at a national or an international level, but ultimately its greatest benefits will come from the close involvement of local social partners, those who will closely represent employers, workmates and fellow citizens.

b.

The fact that each of the initiatives is composed of collaborators who were not working together until present levels of unemployment and the radical changes forced upon people in terms of their expectations of work, and in terms of their appreciation of how they must prepare themselves for it, obliged them to seek **fresh approaches and new professional partners**. This has shown a remarkable consistency in the acceptance of the need for change, and often ability to respond quickly and creatively beyond what might have been expected. One of its important by-products has been the creation of networks of common effort and understanding which are likely to be of great significance in future, not just for the education and training of young people, but for the development of improved approaches to continuing adult education, training and retraining.

c.

The fact that in each case it is recognized, even if it is not fully reflected in all of the work, that young people's transition to work is part of a **much larger and more important process** of transition to adult life. In fact there are many cases when the positive steps designed to help young people find and retain jobs fail to work as they should because other problems like housing or family difficulties have not been dealt with. For many young people the great changes in their prospects of work are partly symptoms of far greater and more general social change, and are partly its cause. The real purpose of local coordination is to be able to recognize this fact, and to provide a practical response to it. Among the difficulties which those responsible for local initiatives face is the preference at national level for the compartmentalization of problems and services: a process which makes it easier to control expenditure and more straightforward to evaluate in statistical terms. For this reason the initiatives which are directly reflected in this handbook are divided between those for whom a breadth of responsibility is part of their nationally-agreed brief, and those for whom the agreed brief is narrower, but who achieve a broad and integrated response to young people's problems as a result of working (and often informal) arrangements. The most complete examples of initiatives formally charged with a broad response to young people's problems are the French *missions locales,* coordinated from the Délégation Interministérielle à l'Insertion Professionnelle et Sociale des Jeunes en Difficulté. The most complete example of a locally-generated initiative is the Oberhausen Verbundsystem.

4.1.2. Examination of these different initiatives leads to the conclusion that:

It should be a firm objective throughout the Community to ensure that all young people — not just those who have been identified as at risk or already in difficulty, or suffering from some distinct handicap or disadvantage — have access to an integrated range of transitional services organized as far as possible within the context of local needs and local resources. The twin objectives of the undoubted effort which must be put into the integration of educational, vocational, social and personal services should be accepted as:

a.
to provide young people with the best and most comprehensive means of preparing themselves to organize their lives in the context of rapidly-changing economic and social conditions;

b.
to guarantee the most cost-effective use of the wide and complex range of services and opportunities available to young people by seeing to it that they are delivered in a complementary manner, and that their use is sufficiently well-organized to eliminate, where possible, instances where a particular educational or training opportunity is wasted on a young person who is unable to take proper advantage of it because a social or personal difficulty exists and has not been given expert attention.

4.2. The needs of young people

In a time of rapid and radical change there is no more important investment to be made than that which helps people to understand what is happening and gives them the opportunity to respond to it in an organized and dignified manner. Young people are sufficiently intelligent and aware to understand that no one knows exactly what is going to happen to the job markets of the European Community in the next few years. They realize that their immediate employment prospects are uncertain, and in many cases they are bad. But they also know that some things are worth doing. The numbers in which they apply themselves to education and training opportunities confirm that they realize that it is sensible for them to invest in their own skills and abilities. At the same time they expect, and they have a right to expect that what they do is treated entirely seriously, and is resourced as a major investment in the future economic and social fabric of the European Community. They have a particular right to expect:

4.2.1. That every effort will be made to provide them with easy access to information and to whatever advice they need. This must cover education, training, employment and social and personal issues. Without it they cannot be expected to understand or to make proper use of the wide — but frequently changing — range of opportunities and facilities which local and national authorities everywhere are devising to counter the effects of unemployment, technological change and the demand for new forms of training.

4.2.2. That everything possible will be done to ensure the immediate as well as the long-term relevance of what they learn and do. In other words, that it is designed with the full range of local employment opportunities in mind, and that it equips them with relevant, recognized skills, and also the opportunity to return later either to education or to training in order to add further skills.

4.2.3. That those who organize training and other services, and the trainers themselves, are fully and properly trained, so that even the most basic training is an experience of high quality. In fact it should be realized that the highest quality is most needed in the most basic training. It is most needed by young people who have failed at school or who have been failed by the education system.

4.2.4. That it be understood that the question of their social and material status is of real importance. It is not that young people want a status they do not merit, nor that they expect excessive rewards. The anger many of them feel about these things is only partly to do with quantities of money. It is far more to do with consistency of attitude and treatment.

Young people do not understand why in some Member States if they choose one kind of education or training at the age of 16 they may receive no payment at all, whereas if they choose another (usually some new form of training) they receive a wage or allowance. They are told that it is difficult to make the changes to ensure that there is consistency, but they find it hard to believe that it is impossible. It seems more likely either that the issue has very low priority with governments, or that they are too confused themselves about the status of young people and the role they are expected to play in society to be able to make any decision.

4.2.5. The major conclusions from these points relating to the status of young people are that Member States, and where appropriate the European Community, should attach high priority to:

a.
Clarifying the status of young people during their period of transition. This includes specifying whether or not transitional status begins during compulsory schooling. It includes forming a view on when transitional status ends.

b.
Recognizing that clarification by some uniformity (first within Member States, later perhaps on a Community basis) in the rights and rewards which young people acquire during this time. Young people themselves would probably favour some formula based upon needs and responsibilities, varied with a significant reward factor.

c.
A clear specification at both Member State and Community levels of the expectations which young people themselves are entitled to have during this period of transition. These would include:

● much improved access to information and advice about the complexities of the obligations and choices they face; information in particular, should be provided far more in the form of an open resource, than in the form it so often now takes of a specific and privileged input made when those who provide the information think it most appropriate; in many respects this is the most important recommendation of all, because without it nothing else can be done as well or as efficiently; by far the best results will be gained from the provision of information and advice at a single accessible, local venue;

● a clear expectation about the range of educational and vocational choice available; this would have to be linked both to the realities of educational and training provision available nationally, and also to the confirmed potential of local provision;

● a clear commitment to concentrate all measures primarily on the acquisition of employment; young people want to succeed, and they want to be trained with the skills to succeed; training without work to follow is of value, but it cannot be denied that it involves in every case a damaging rupture of expectations and a waste of ability;

● further use of national and Community funds to ensure that young people have reasonable equality of opportunity regardless of where they live; this means that extra effort and expenditure is required in locations where existing educational and training infrastructure is widely dispersed or inadequate — rural areas, underfunded inner-cities;

● clear statements in all Member States of their practical guarantees of personal equality of opportunity during transition;

● a role, especially at a local level in both co-determining the programmes available to them, and also in participating as far as possible in their management and administration.

4.3. Local planning

Local planning of the use of both local and national resources is effective in designing initiatives which match the preferences of young people to the real opportunities on the job market. This is not to ignore the need for national standards of training and vocational education; much progress has been made in most Member States towards improving and updating the training curricula. But job opportunities for young people tend to reflect the needs of small and medium-sized enterprises, or even the initiative of the young people themselves. If these opportunities are to be served by training — which in many cases is the most significant single investment which can be made — the training must be administered flexibly, and capable of being adapted as close to individual needs as possible. Local planning and administration is the most cost-effective approach because it ensures the highest degree of relevance for all that is taught. To be effective it requires:

4.3.1. That Member States and the Community take all possible steps to encourage the development of local planning and coordination of educational, training and advisory services for young people.

In some Member States the machinery for doing this is already in place. In others it is a matter of encouragement (financial and general) and of ensuring that what is known of successful methods of coordination are well-known and understood. This is a topic on which the European Commission, through Cedefop, can play an important role by publicizing and encouraging the analysis and further refinement of good practice.

4.3.2. That those responsible for planning at a local level have access to good economic and social information. Without this, initiatives are likely to be instituted without proper regard to local circumstances.

4.3.3. That Member States recognize that the labour market will not — in the medium-term at any rate — adjust itself to accommodate young people. Adjustments will take place over the long-term, but in the meantime there is no alternative to major initiatives both in training and in job-creation by public authorities.

4.3.4. At the level of local government, it is important that there is integration at least of information about economic, educational and social policies affecting young people. Some form of more formal political coordination of the policies which affect young people is desirable, and where it is achieved will yield significant benefits in the form of improved relevance and quality of what is done, and will therefore be cost-effective. Above all everyone must know what role he or she is supposed to be playing. There is too much duplication of effort, too little clarity of responsibility.

4.3.5. Both at the level of national and of local governments there should be a formal requirement on agencies providing services for young people to undertake a measure of local coordination of their activities with each other. Again this will save rather than cost money by improving the efficiency with which young people make use of services. It will also greatly decrease the overlap between the activities of different agencies, making them more relevant, and enabling them to learn from each other to improve the quality of what they do.

4.3.6. Further than this, there are obvious benefits from the establishment of multi-disciplinary teams to plan individual education, training and social projects. Planning undertaken by a mixture of permanent administrators with seconded experts from different agencies and different disciplines is likely to result in highly inventive application of resources to local problems and opportunities.

4.3.7. In ensuring that local plans are both relevant to the needs of young people and also compatible with the pattern of existing provision and with different national structures of education and training, it is important that they are required to be rooted firmly in collaboration not just between the individuals and agencies taking part, but also with others who have contact with young people and responsibility for them before and after they are regarded as being in transition. For this reason the schools must be formally involved in many aspects of the planning, and so must both parents and employers. When young people move from compulsory education to transition programmes, and when they move from transition programmes to work, it is vital that their needs are understood and catered for as far as possible, and also that their strengths and abilities are fully appreciated and are strongly and fully represented to employers.

4.4. Non-industrial and rural areas

A major concern for the European Community and for Member States is the development of effective means of providing programmes for young people who live in **non-industrialized and rural areas.** The priority for this is emphasized by the accession to the European Community of Spain and Portugal, and also by the swift rate of change in many rural areas in other Member States.

Actions should include:

4.4.1. A concerted programme of practical exchange of relevant experience and collaborative development of new training and employment creation techniques between professionals working in non-industrialized and rural areas in **all Member States.** This should result in a bank of information and practical models, available alike to public authorities, to business and to individuals.

4.4.2. Special studies on potential employment and enterprise-creation activities, especially those making use of redundant or under-used premises and equipment, and those depending on new technology. Additional studies to clarify the best means of training young people for these activities.

4.4.3. Actions to encourage and assist potential promoters of training and employment creation activities in non-industrialized and rural areas to make full use of Community financial instruments, by more active publicity for currently successful initiatives, and by the promotion of the development between Member States of 'common dossiers' (applications for parallel initiatives in different Member States).

The phenomenon of high youth unemployment has been caused by two converging forces: technological and structural change in all European economies and in their relationship to the economies not just of the USA and Japan but to those of other developed and underdeveloped countries; and increased supplies of actual and potential labour caused by the presence of large cohorts of young people in the population of nearly all Member States, and by the increased desire amongst women in some Member States to take full or part-time employment.

In most Member States there are signs that the overall number of young people seeking training will decrease and will be somewhat smaller by the 1990s. **This must not be taken to mean that unemployment among young people will necessarily fall either in proportional or in real terms. There is no evidence to suggest that this will happen.**

It is essential that both Member States and the Community as a whole should be clear that:

4.5.1. Whereas demand for basic training for young people will decrease, the other element of the training which has been developed for young people in the last few years — training for change, and particularly training to help people respond to changing economic circumstances — will continue to be in demand. In addition the cohorts of young people who have left compulsory education since 1979 (and before that in some Member States) and who have been affected throughout by unemployment, will continue to need extra resources and assistance for much of their working lives. It is likely that many of them will remain highly vulnerable to both social and economic change. **The coordinated services, especially of information and advice which have been developed for young people, must be confirmed in place and further developed to meet the needs of the 1990s by ensuring that the process of basic training and personal development is carried on into adult life in the form of a continuing access to the services and to the knowledge necessary to living and working in a changing society.**

4.5.2. In addition, fresh resources must be dedicated to the development of new employment of all kinds to ensure that all young people have the opportunity to play a useful part in society, and to possess the independence which goes with a job. The labour market will not provide these jobs. Only a partnership between the public and private sectors and young people themselves can do this. Only a genuine integration of the local services and resources necessary to the process can ensure that it is done efficiently, and at a reasonable cost in both human and financial terms.

Essential data

Contents

1

The initatives

Business School/Technical School-Randers
DK

VEC and AnCO Cork
IRL

COA Limburg
NL

Sussex Training (West)
UK

Verbundsystem Oberhausen
D

Mission Locale Lorient
F

Mission Locale La Rochelle
F

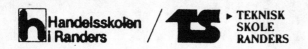

Summary

The cooperation between the Business School and the Technical School in Randers ensures the legal obligation which exists in Denmark to assist young people between the ages of 16 and 18 with their transition from school to work, even when they have left the compulsory schooling system.

The system of advice and counselling is provided in close collaboration with local social partners.

Background

Denmark is divided into 14 counties and two metropolitan boroughs, Copenhagen and Fredericksberg which to a large extent have the same administrative status as the counties. The country is further divided into 275 municipalities. This administrative division is of particular importance for the organization of education in the primary and lower secondary school (Folkeskolen). Municipalities provide education for children of compulsory school age. Randers is an administrative county and has 13 municipalities; one is the town of Randers, in which this initiative is located.

The initiative is based on the Business School of Randers (Handelsskolen i Randers) and the Technical School (Teknisk Skole Randers) where efforts are being made to assist young people in the 16-18 age group throughout the transition from compulsory schooling to work, training and education.

In Denmark a compulsory education period of nine years was introduced in 1972/73. After the 1975 Education Act the two separate systems of primary school and lower secondary school, which had existed up to then, were brought together in the one single school during the entire nine-year compulsory school process. On the completion of the ninth year students have access to the upper school (Gymnasium), the business and technical schools and other training, education and apprenticeships opportunities. It is also possible for students to undertake a 10th year in the compulsory school system.

Entry to the compulsory school system starts at 6/7 years of age. Young people leave the compulsory school system at 15/16 or 16/17 years of age.

Target group

The advice and counselling provided by the coordinated efforts of the two schools is focused largely on the young people who experience unemployment after finishing compulsory schooling. They come from:

The business school	— After completing the one year basic business course approximately 22% of the students are unemployed.
The technical school	— After completing the one year basic technical course nearly 20% are unemployed.
Upper secondary school (sixth form college)	— This is intended for those who may wish to go into higher education. However, some of the students obtain a job or short-term education. Others apply for apprenticeships. About 17% are unemployed after leaving the sixth form college.
Occasional work or no work	— Some young people require unskilled jobs, others temporary jobs whereas another group require apprenticeships. The whole group is registered as applicants for more permanent jobs or apprenticeships.

Approximately 70-80% of the unemployed 16 to 18-year olds apply for jobs as apprentices or trainees. Unemployed young people register for employment at the job centre.

Young people in transition: There are four clear features of the Randers initiative:

(a)

A curriculum-based system of guidance, counselling and information for students — This system covers compulsory schooling, the first year of school in vocational education and unemployment and comprises the following:

First of all, in compulsory school a programme is being developed which covers the eighth, ninth and where appropriate the 10th years. This programme includes the involvement of a school counsellor/form master working with the young person on vocational guidance and covers practical training, work in a factory, practical training in a vocational school, work experience, factory visits, information for teachers, students and parents, open house events and visiting lectures from the Danish Council of Trade Unions and the Federation of Danish Employers.

Second, part of the system relates to the first year of post compulsory school and vocational education. This involves a school counsellor/form master and includes factory visits, vocational guidance, cooperation with the employment service and the 'Liaison Committee'.

Third, if unemployed after leaving the vocational school then contacts with the employment service, the Liaison Committee and the local authority adviser are all part of the continuing process of guidance and counselling.

(b)

Cooperation between education and training systems and social partners and local authority — Within the project there is an acknowledgement of the need to have a 'community' of interests involved in tackling the problems facing young people. As the project is concerned with the creation of more jobs and apprenticeships then it is a vital component of the project that the Trade Unions and the Employers' Associations be directly involved. This close cooperation has formed the basis of the setting up within the initiative of a Liaison Committee.

(c)

The Liaison Committee — In the spring of 1982 Randers took the step of arranging a meeting for the Federation of Danish Employers, the Danish Council of Trade Unions, the local authority of Randers, the Trades Association of Randers, the Job Centre, the Technical School of Randers and the Business School of Randers to discuss the various possibilities of providing more placements for apprentices and trainees.

On that occasion a committee was set up, the Liaison Committee, with the aim of providing more placements for apprentices and trainees. The committee comprised representatives of the above organizations and institutions.

Shortly after this the Danish Vocational Training Directorate announced that grants would be given to provide employment opportunities. All the participants agreed that the two vocational schools should apply jointly for finance to assist with the planned activities of the committee.

The work of the Liaison Committee includes the following:

1.
Providing employment opportunities through visits to firms.
2.
Initiative day for young people applying for jobs as apprentices and trainees.
3.
Meetings for representatives of the labour market.
4.
Advertising campaign.
5.
Making lists of employers.
6.
Job-day for students attending the one-year basic business or technical course.
7.
Information arrangements for smaller groups of employers (trade associations).

The Ministry of Education and the Federation of Danish Employers provide grants to assist with the above activities.

(d)

Temporary measures for young people — The problem of providing jobs for apprentices and trainees has in recent years become more difficult. Unemployment in Denmark has not risen to the high levels experienced in other Member States. Nevertheless numbers have grown, and there have been significant increases in long-term unemployment.

As a result of this, temporary measures, financed from national and local public funds, have been introduced to improve the prospects of young people obtaining permanent jobs. It should be stressed however, that most of the young people involved in such temporary measures are still applying for places as apprentices and trainees. A few of them prefer to take unskilled jobs. These temporary measures for young people are provided on the basis that they are 'waiting for places as apprentices/trainees or unskilled operators'.

There are two schemes. First, an Introductory-vocational course (EIFU) for unemployed young people which lasts for nine weeks and is succeeded by four practical weeks in industry. The course centre organizes this practical work. The young people receive financial suport from public funds and the scheme involves young people who are both under and over 18 years of age. Second, employment schemes run by the local authority. These projects vary in number from area to area and usually cater for the long-term unemployed. Most of the projects are based on some form of **production** and it is stressed that these projects must not take away work from existing firms in the area in the form of job substitution. The young people work in the projects for a period of nine months, and receive a wage. It is however acknowledged that few young people find work after their nine months on the project. The projects nevertheless are designed to create 'good working habits'. In particular they are aimed at those young people who find it difficult to enter the labour market.

The principles behind the work

The initiative is based on clearly identified objectives and seeks to put greater effort into innovation within the existing pattern of jobs and training options so as to enable young people to have a greater range of opportunities. There is an emphasis on assisting young people to use existing opportunities to the maximum. At the same time attempts are being made to create more training places and apprenticeships within the local area. There is therefore less concern with developing a wider range of innovatory schemes for the unemployed outside the mainstream of traditional work and training opportunities.

The following considerations underpin the work being done in Randers.

(a)
There is an emphasis on organizing, advising and counselling young people to help them take advantage of available opportunities in the Randers area.

(b)
An extensive curriculum-based guidance, counselling and information process which starts with the compulsory school, continues through post compulsory training and education to unemployment.

(c)
By using the knowledge of the labour market, the needs of the local economy and the particular requirements of local firms it is hoped that more opportunities for young people can be obtained.

(d)
The initiative emphasizes the importance of the social partners and the need to create links between them, local government, the job centre and the business and technical schools — an emphasis on creating a wider responsibility for the plight of the young unemployed.

(e)

There is an emphasis on the concept of motivating young people and retaining their interest in the conventional work environment. Even in relation to the special measures there is an emphasis on work discipline and the fact that unemployment is just a break in the transition from the school to adult and working life.

(f)

There is an optimistic and positive advocacy of the qualities of young people. Particular emphasis is given to their desire to work and to make a contribution to society. These directly or indirectly create the impression within young people of hope and confidence in the future and as a result this will hopefully influence in a positive way, the perception of the youth problem held by the community.

(g)

The emphasis on generating enthusiasm and confidence, maintaining expectations and the development of positive attitudes on the part of young people — acknowledging as it does the social, emotional and psychological problems which can emerge through a period of long-term unemployment.

(h)

The concept of the Liaison Committee which extends in a positive way the concept that the responsibility for helping young people and providing jobs must be shared by the wider community.

(i)

An emphasis on the traditional job and apprenticeship system where objectives clearly reflect the history and traditions of the Danish economy, the training and education systems and the needs and expectations of young people; but increasingly reflects a situation where the needs and aspirations of young people are more difficult to satisfy as technological change accelerates and unemployment grows.

(j)

Less emphasis on non-traditional innovatory schemes for the young unemployed and a greater emphasis on guidance and counselling aimed at helping young people use available opportunities more effectively — equipping young people in a better form of self-management and self-development in relation to the choices which might be available to them.

VERBUNDSYSTEM OBERHAUSEN

Summary

The Oberhausen network is a local initiative in this part of the Ruhr coordinating the range of educational, training and guidance facilities available to young people who leave school and are unable to find education, training or work places, and finding ways of developing new opportunities.

History and structure

Oberhausen has a population of approximately 235 000 and is located in the western part of the Ruhr area in North Rhine-Westphalia. Oberhausen is a classical example of a community with a tradition for coal mining and steel production.

Over the last 20 years, several thousand jobs have been lost in the traditional industries and it was only possible to offset a small percentage by way of an expansion of public services. Since the late 1970s, Oberhausen has experienced above-average unemployment, in particular amongst young people.

A whole range of practical education and training programmes have been introduced since the mid 1970s with the objective of providing those young people who upon leaving school had been unable to find a job or a training place, with the possibility of attaining qualifications through vocational preparation measures or, alternatively, preparing them for a future occupation by extending their term at school. In the late 1970s both the *Länder* and the labour authorities had developed numerous practical programmes which urgently required reconciliation and coordination. In 1976, a local 'youth unemployment working group' was established.

In the early 1980s it became clear that bridging measures and training programmes could not provide a real solution to the problem, but that it was essential to create more extensive training and employment measures. With the support of the municipality of Oberhausen, under the joint responsibility of almost all the relevant institutional establishments in Oberhausen, an independent training centre was created. In the early 1980s some 600 young people benefited from the various vocational preparation and training measures. It became evident from the technical, organizational and political point of view there was a need for better coordination and planning of the Oberhausen network.

In 1985 the Oberhausen network had three essential functions:

(a)

the political and management function;

(b)

the financial and organizational function;

(c)

the technical function.

It comprises:

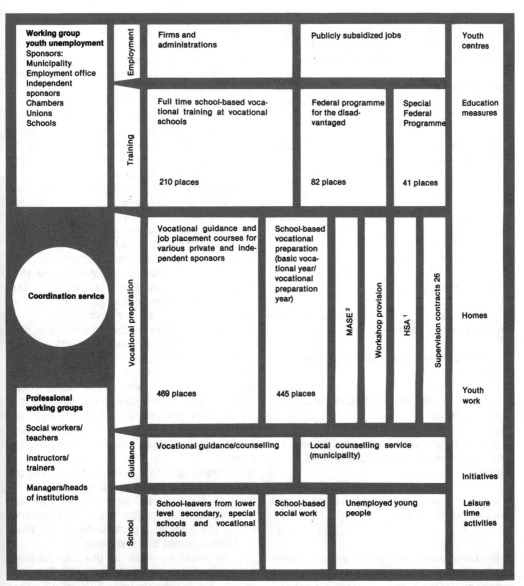

| | | Employment | Firms and administrations | | Publicly subsidized jobs | | Youth centres |

(figure continued)

| Working group youth unemployment | | Employment | Firms and administrations | Publicly subsidized jobs | | Youth centres |

Working group youth unemployment
Sponsors:
Municipality
Employment office
Independent sponsors
Chambers
Unions
Schools

Coordination service

Professional working groups

Social workers/teachers

Instructors/trainers

Managers/heads of institutions

Employment — Firms and administrations / Publicly subsidized jobs / Youth centres

Training — Full time school-based vocational training at vocational schools — 210 places / Federal programme for the disadvantaged — 82 places / Special Federal Programme — 41 places / Education measures

Vocational preparation — Vocational guidance and job placement courses for various private and independent sponsors — 469 places / School-based vocational preparation (basic vocational year/vocational preparation year) — 445 places / MASE [2] / Workshop provision / HSA [1] / Supervision contracts 26 / Homes / Youth work

Guidance — Vocational guidance/counselling / Local counselling service (municipality) / Initiatives

School — School-leavers from lower level secondary, special schools and vocational schools / School-based social work / Unemployed young people / Leisure time activities

[1] School-leaving certificate courses.
[2] Measures for the vocational preparation and social integration of young people.

Work with young people between school and working life

The target group of the Oberhausen network covers all young people up to 20 years of age, and in some cases beyond, who have not found employment or a training place.

For in-company and non-school-based measures, action is focused on the group of so-called 'disadvantaged young people'.

- school-leavers or drop-outs from the lower secondary and special schools and young people completing the basic vocational training year;

- drop-outs from training and other measures;

- juvenile delinquents;

- potential drug addicts;

- young people with a serious lack of motivation and low stamina;

- young people from socially problematic or broken families;

- young people from homes and residential groups;

- young girls (even if the proportion with better educational qualifications is often high);

- young foreigners, who often have language difficulties.

In the Oberhausen network there are basically five elements. Whilst the sector **school/school social work** concentrates on school-leavers from lower secondary, special and vocational schools, it also includes elements of social and education work for young people outside the schools and of course includes work with young people who have already completed compulsory schooling and are unemployed.

Whilst a large number of young people benefit from the **guidance and counselling** of the local employment office, which begins at school and from there is extended to cover existing occupations and training opportunities, the local guidance centre of the municipality of Oberhausen devotes itself primarily to those young people who for reasons of their family situation and their social and educational disadvantages are, for the time being, unable to find a job or a training place. A special guidance service also exists for young foreigners and this service works in cooperation with the schools and offers guidance to young foreigners in almost every relevant field.

The main element in the Oberhausen network is that of **vocational preparation.** Over 1 100 places are provided, accounting for more than 2/3 of all the practical measures of the network system. In this sector vocational guidance and placement courses run by various private and independent organizations, and the school-based vocational preparation measures are clearly predominant.

In the **training** sector, efforts are focused on increasing the local training capacity by way of full-time school-based vocational training and off-the-job vocational training under the special programmes of the Federal Government and the *Land.*

The smallest element in the Oberhausen network relates to **additional jobs.** This accounts for approximateley 10% of all existing places in the Oberhausen network and offers far too few practical possibilities for young people to prove their practical abilities after participating in vocational training measures.

Contact is established with the young people for the various measures at four levels:

- cooperation between the various organizations and the schools;
- through the three existing counselling services;
- through cooperation amongst the various organizations;
- through personal contacts with the young people and their parents.

Structure and quality of local coordination

The following chart illustrates the efforts which have been made in respect of cooperation and coordination of the various measures at a local level. So far the municipal guidance and counselling service and a member of the staff of an independent institution have been taking care of the coordination function on a decentralized basis. Long-term this function is to be equipped with appropriate decision-making and technical competencies.

Decision-making and counselling structures in the Oberhausen network

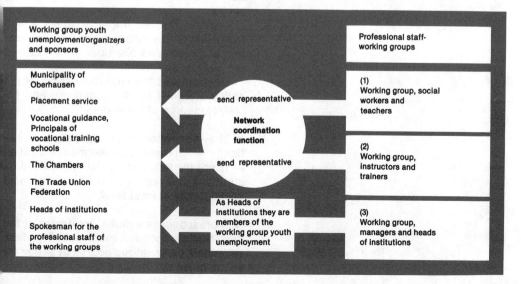

'Missions locales' for the transition of young people to adult and working life: Lorient and La Rochelle, F

Summary

The *missions locales* in Lorient and La Rochelle are two examples of a network of 100 local centres placed in areas of high unemployment in France. They are the result of a collaboration on one level between the central government and local authorities, and on another between the social partners and a wide range of educational, training and social agencies. They provide a focus of advice and assistance for young people with any problems they experience, not just those directly connected with employment, and they also serve as catalysts and animators of new forms of provision for young people.

At national level, the *missions locales* are aided by supporting and flanking measures undertaken by the interministerial delegation for the vocational and social integration of youth in difficulty, which is under the supervision of the prime minister and headed by a 'délégué interministeriel'.

mission locale
pour l'insertion sociale et professionnelle des jeunes

Historical background of the 'mission locales'

September 1981: Publication of Professor Bertrand Schwartz's report.
'The vocational and social integration of youth', this is the title of a report written by Professor Bertrand Schwartz at the request of the prime minister. This report envisages a package of emergency and longer-term measures involving the **mobilization** at local level of all social, economic, administrative and political forces.

September 1982: The government proposes a number of new approaches for the vocational integration and qualification of youth. In the areas with the largest number of young persons in difficulty (with no training and no qualification) *missions locales* for the integration of the young are established at the request of the local authority concerned.

The local deputies, the public services, the associations and the economic and social partners join together and try to devise solutions for the problems of these young people.

Altogether, the geographical areas which they cover represent one-fifth of the population of France and one quarter of youth in the 16 to 26 age group.

Two hypotheses form the foundation for the policy designed for the vocational and social integration of the young.

● The integration of young people in difficulty — if it merits specific measures at all — is not the sole concern of specialized institutions but requires the **mobilization of social forces at local level.**

● It presupposes a **global treatment** of the problems of youth and the possibility of **developing a personalized course of action** for young persons.

The option of fitting this policy into a **local framework** follows directly from this approach. The objective here is to:

- reduce the gap between youth and the institutions and between the institutions themselves.

- tackle the problems of youth on the basis of their specific local situations.

The *missions locales* are the concrete result of these options and they are part of the process of **decentralization** of the State's powers to regional and local level.

Functions and structure of the 'missions locales'

The *mission locale* is the place where the **mobilization** of all local partners is undertaken in order to provide a **global response** to the problems of youth in the 16-26 age group.

The *missions locales* try to solve not only the problems of training and employment, but also to improve other aspects of their day-to-day lives: housing, health, recreation, sports, culture.

They also act as a catalyst for the public schemes designed for young persons, and are the most suitable places for coordination and innovation.

The *missions locales* originality and their **raison d'être** stem from four main factors:

- **Their ambition:** to tackle the whole set of problems confronting young persons and to follow up the fate of these young persons until they can take their lives into their own hands.

- **The inter-institutional nature of their activities:** The *missions locales* are founded on the initiative of the local authorities who also provide half of their resources, while the other half comes from the State (Vocational Training, Social Advancement and Employment Funds).

They are organized as an **association** based on the situation prevailing in that area; the Management Board of the *missions locales* consists of all voluntary participants in the economic and social life of the area: local deputies, administrators, associations, employers' and employees' organizations. An Executive Committee (Bureau) consisting of about a dozen members, is the executive body of the association. It prepares the budget and sees that it is implemented.

The aim of the *missions locales* is to 'work with' and to 'work differently' but not to do the job of existing institutions. Their purpose is to improve the efficiency of existing private and public structures whose activities, often fragmentary, require coordination at local level.

● The inter-disciplinary nature of the technical team which supports the association.

● One of the main objectives of the *missions locales* is to function as an instrument of innovation and experimentation because, by definition, their activities are directed towards young persons for whom the classical solutions do not provide the right answer.

The *missions locales* try to develop — in cooperation with all local partners — new and original initiatives promoting the integration of youth into the framework of a **local economic and social development policy.**

The Management Board is chaired by the mayor of the leading municipality in the geographical area concerned and, in some cases, by the Chairman of the Intermunicipal Association *(Syndicat intercommunal).*

The technical team which is assigned the task of implementing the policy established by the Management Board, is made up of at least 12 persons, half of whom are salaried employees of the association and half of whom are seconded from the administrations of other authorities (National educa-

tion, social services, ANPE, AFPA, etc.). The technical team is directed by a coordinator (who is a woman in more than one-third of the *missions locales).*

It ensures direct contact with young persons and monitors their training and their integration.

Financing — the cost

The financing of the *missions locales* is undertaken jointly by the State and the regional, departmental and local authorities.

The main resources come from the grants provided by the Vocational Training and Social Advancement Funds and from the subsidies and contributions in kind (staff, premises) from the regional, departmental and local authorities. To this one may add the resources originating from various administrations, in particular the Ministry of Women's Rights, the Social Action for Migrant Workers' Fund, the Ministry of Agriculture, etc.; these take the form either of specific services (vocational guidance modules, for example) or of schemes geared to the specific situations of some youth groups (women, rural youth, migrants).

In 1984 the total budgetary expenditure of the 86 *missions locales* who were in existence on 1 January 1984 rose to FF 100.5 million, 42.7 million of which were given by the Vocational Training and Social Advancement Funds. These subsidies rose by 5% (current value) from 1983 to 1984.

The average budgetary expenditure for the *missions locales* in 1984 amounted to FF 1 160 000, there were, however, considerable variations depending on the *mission locale* concerned (from 1 to 5).

The 'mission locale' for the future of youth in the Lorient area

Set up in September 1982 on the initiative of the town of Lorient, the *mission locale* of the Lorient area today (end of 1985) serves 20 municipalities; its geographical sphere of action covers a population of about 200 000 inhabitants.

The Management Board consists of 12 mayors, 12 representatives of public administrations, 12 representatives of economic and social bodies, and 12 private and public training establishments and institutions.

The Chairman of the association is Deputy-Mayor of the town of Lorient. The coordination of the multi-disciplinary technical team, which consists of 12 permanent members, is in the hands of Jean-Luc le Clech (an official from the Ministry of Education).

In the two and a half years of its existence the *mission locale* has received more than 3 000 young people in its different reception centres (12) located in the municipalities of the catchment area for employment.

The breakdown of the age structure of these 3 000 young persons is as follows:

- 25% are 16 to 18 years old;
- 50% are 18 to 21 years old;
- 25% are 21 to 26 years old.

The educational level of these young persons is poor and more than 60% have no qualification at all.

The 'mission locale' of La Rochelle

Location
Number of inhabitants: 119 210
Number of cantons: 6 urban cantons, 5 rural cantons
Number of municipalities: 57

The association 'mission locale'

Date of establishment of the association: October 1982

Composition of the Management Board:

elected representatives: the mayors of member municipalities are statutory members plus
six elected representatives of La Rochelle
administrations: 12 members
associations: 17 members
trainers: 11 members
social partners: six representatives (three for the employers, three for the employees)

Composition of the Executive Committee: its task is to see that the decisions of the Management Board are implemented, prepare meetings, examine the 'day-to-day life' of the association. It consists of seven members of the Management Board.

Composition of the technical team: it consists of persons who are responsible for the routine operations of the *mission locale:* salaried staff and staff members seconded by the administrations. (National education, social services, employment, justice, La Rochelle town, women's rights).

Categories of target groups

Quantitative breakdown for the **arrondissement** of La Rochelle:

- Unemployed youth make up 45% of job-seekers
- Almost all young persons in the age group 16-18 come to the *mission locale* (300 per year)
- One out of four young persons in the age group 18-26 come to the *mission locale*
- In the last three years the *mission locale* has received some 3 000 young people

Lorient and La Rochelle:
The main tasks of the 'mission locale'

Objectives

Define the situations and the needs of youth aged 16 to 25 with no employment and no training in the Lorient catchment area for employment.

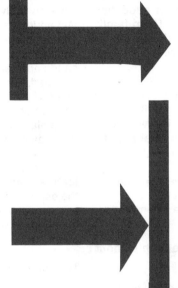

Induce appropriate responses from the local partners.

Functions

Receive, inform, guide and monitor the progress of young persons.

Draw up plans for the provision of training and the organization of training courses for youth.

Support initiatives for the creation of employment by and for youth.

Support projects which will develop the social environment of youth (health, housing, recreation, holidays).

Support projects aimed at developing the expression of youth.

The young — Who are they?

In qualitative terms the problems are the following:

For the 16-18 year-olds, the predominant problem is the very low level of education (58% have had no training). Their family situations are very similar to the results of the CEREQ national survey which showed that:

● 83% of the young persons come from large families (more than three children), of these 68% come from families with four children and more (7% of the total population);

● 16% come from single-parent families;

● 42% have fathers who are unemployed, absent or deceased;

● 28% have parents who are both without employment;

● 70% come from a working class environment, most of them are non-qualified.

These figures vary depending on the category of the youth group concerned and they are strongly correlated with the low level of schooling.

In the 18-26 age group the social situation is less adverse; the dropouts from school are no longer in the majority. Those who have completed their normal schooling join the ranks of the job-seekers, and their social origin is similar to that of the traditional French population. However, the majority of those who come to the *mission locale* are the most under-privileged within this group. A recent survey shows that in the La Rochelle conurbation 73% of the youth received in the *mission locale* come from working class districts.

The needs of the young

Fact: Youth is not 'one' set of persons, there are as many different situations as there are individuals. Because of this, it is necessary — and this does not simplify the task — to have an individual orientation of methods and actions.

The population that comes to the *missions locales* is a population with accumulated handicaps, stigmatized in school, socially deprived, and because of all this, faced with real difficulties in its vocational and social integration; the low probability of employment plus the accumulated handicaps force it into an economic context which is particularly difficult.

This population may present some common features, but the individual histories and the personal situations are very diverse, and are especially more marked when it is a question of young people living in rural areas.

The main common features are:

● their passiveness (little capacity to take personal initiatives, few or no precise wishes), their behaviour is that of mere customers;
● a lack of focus (in space and in time).

The main demands of the young

● First and foremost, **employment** — 'anything, whatever it may be, but as fast as possible' — in order to obtain an income for living. This demand is the main concern of those with diplomas and above all, of those over 18.

● **Training** — This demand is mostly expressed by those who are drop-outs from school and is the major concern of those in the 16-18 age group. However, many young persons above the age of 18 also wish to get training (either re-training or complementary training to follow up their initial training). This demand often masks the failure to find a job.

Among the young persons undergoing training several motivations may be identified:

(a) the desire for training;
(b) the desire to defer action (they are waiting for . . .)
(c) the desire for vocational accomplishment;
(d) necessity.

● **Social aids** — The demands for aid for non- vocational needs are growing. These young persons are sinking deeper and deeper into a state of financial distress. Unemployment sometimes lasts for more than a year, especially among the girls.

Organization of local resources

The *mission locale* tries to encourage a strategy of action and concertation among local partners (private and public); it does not have the intention of administering resources on behalf of any other organization.

The *mission locale* therefore, promotes joint action of local agents in a specific field or in a project.

In addition to the organizational bodies of the *mission locale* (General Assembly, Management Board and Executive Committee) there are also three working groups (employment/training, social economy and daily life). The institutions, the economic and social partners, the training establishments and the associations divide the tasks amongst themselves in keeping with their specific responsibilities.

A distinction must be made between two types of local partners:

● the partners in the field with whom the *mission local* conducts joint schemes oriented towards youth. They are operational partners (training establishments, associations, local administrations, local authorities, etc.),

● the decision-making partners who are to be found in the local, departmental and regional bodies and who are often the funders (State, General Council, Regional Council).

The *mission locale,* therefore, works together with almost a hundred local partners and induces them to implement schemes for the benefit of young persons facing the greatest difficulties; these schemes are a part of the framework established at national or regional level but are adapted to the specific features of the catchment area (social and economic environment, situation of youth, etc.).

Despite all this, the fact remains that the development of concertation structures by the local partners is a slow process and will continue to be one. Also, the vertical organization of the institutions is not very conducive to innovation.

Cork Vocational Education Committee and AnCO, the Industrial Training Authority, IRL

comtec

Summary

The Vocational Education Committee, responsible for a high proportion of secondary and vocational education in the city, and AnCO, the Industrial Training Authority, which is responsible for a wide range of basic and specific vocational training programmes, are among the leading agencies in the provision of services for young people. Apart from informal cooperation, which has developed over a number of years, both are now closely involved in the pilot Comtec, which is designed to lead to greater coordination of their activities and of those of other agencies.

Background

Cork has a population of approximately 150 000 within the city boundary with an additional 100 000 in close proximity and is the second largest city in the Republic of Ireland. Although the initiatives are conceived largely within the Vocational Education Committee area — which corresponds exactly with the boundary of the local authority, Cork County Borough Council — this description acknowledges some of the implications of what is happening in Cork County which has a total population, including that of the City of Cork and its immediate environs, of nearly 400 000. Cork County has a separate Vocational Education Committee and Local Authority.

The education system

In Ireland, children are required to remain in school until they are 15 years old. The primary or **first level** schooling is structured in such a way that by the time the children are 12/13 they have completed the first level of their education. At the **second level** of education in Cork there are four main types of school which children may attend.

The principal differences between the four types of second-level school relate to their forms of management. The secondary schools are generally owned and managed by religious denominations. Vocational schools are owned and managed by Vocational Education Committees (VECs).

Community schools are managed by boards representative of VECs, religious denominations, parents and teachers, while the comprehensive schools are managed by boards representative of VECs, religious denominations and the Department of Education.

Since the mid-1960s, all types of school have provided courses which lead to the same set of certificates and examinations, but there are differences in emphasis. This is probably most marked in the attention given to an academic type of education in the secondary schools, and the more extensive provision of practical forms of education in the vocational schools. Comprehensive and community schools were first established after the mid-1960s, and these schools offer a fully comprehensive range of subjects.

Since young people can leave school any time after the age of 15, the education attainments of children of the same age vary considerably. The period of schooling may vary and also the level of examination achievement.

The great majority of children continue their schooling after the junior cycle into either a two-year senior cycle programme leading to a Leaving Certificate, or a vocational preparation and training programme.

The **third level** of education is concerned with higher full-time education. The major category of student are those in university and regional technical colleges (one of which is located in Cork), and colleges of technology, national institutions of higher education and teacher training colleges.

Organizational context of the education and training systems — national, intermediary and local

1.
The following national government departments have an involvement in the organizing, financing and delivery of programmes for young people:

Department of Education,
Department of Labour,
Department of the Environment,
Department of Agriculture.

2.
AnCO — The Industrial Training Authority* which was established in 1967 to provide for the training of persons for the purposes of any activity of industry and to promote, facilitate, encourage, assist, coordinate and develop the provision of such training. AnCO has wide ranging powers to encourage, promote and provide training for industry through its own training centres and training advisory staff, in association with education agencies and through externally contracted work. Operationally AnCO activities can be described under

Initiatives

These initiatives are available to young people:

1.

Schemes administered by education agencies

Most education agencies are principally concerned with the provision of mainstream education programmes at first, second and third levels and heretofore the provision of vocational training programmes within the education system was carried out largely by the Vocational Education Committees (VECs). The City of Cork VEC is established under the Vocational Education Act 1930 and is involved, *inter alia,* in a range of educational, vocational preparation and training programmes to prepare young people for work and adult life. The Committee is also involved in the provision of mainstream secondary and third-level education courses.

From September 1984 there has been a massive expansion in vocational preparation courses within the education system and these are being provided by all types of school although the greatest numbers of such courses are still provided by VEC schools.

These are provided at two levels:

(a)

One and two-year courses for those who have completed the junior cycle programme of second-level education at about 15 years of age and who are not proceeding to the succeeding two-year course which leads to the Leaving Certificate examinations.

(b)

One-year courses for those who have com-

three headings — apprenticeship training, training for individuals (excluding apprentices) and training within companies. A major AnCO training centre is located in Cork.

3.

CERT — the Council for Education, Recruitment and Training in the hotel and catering industry* — provides initial and in-service training for the hotel, catering and tourism industry through vocational colleges and schools, and through its own training service and advisory agencies.

4.

The **National Manpower Service*** (NMS) is a division of the Department of Labour with responsibility for job placement and for the administration of a wide variety of government employment schemes. The service has a network of offices located throughout the country and one of its eight regional offices is located in Cork.

5.

The **Youth Employment Agency*** (YEA) was established in 1982 to provide for the training and employment of young people. The agency is required to act under the Minister for Labour as the body with overall national responsibility for the furtherance of the employment of young persons and its functions include responsibility for the establishment, development, extension, operation, assistance, encouragement, supervision, coordination and integration, either directly or indirectly, of schemes for the training and employment of young persons.

---

* It should be noted that in September 1986, the Minister for Labour announced plans for the merging of AnCO, CERT, the National Manpower Service and the Youth Employment Agency, but the impact of this on the programmes and activities offered was not clear at the time of publication of this handbook.

pleted the full second-level education programme at about 17 years of age.

All participants in the above programmes are paid an allowance of IRL 300 per year.

Arising from the agreed decisions of the Ministers for Education and Labour referred to in the next section of this description, **arrangements are being made for more extensive interaction between all education agencies and the agencies of the Department of Labour, and these will provide for the education agencies to undertake a far greater proportion of the work involved in preparing young people for entry to adult life and working life.**

2.
Schemes administered by Department of Labour agencies

National Manpower Services

I
Work experience programme: WEP

Employers are encouraged to take on for experience, as additional staff, young unemployed people, under 25 years of age with no previous employment experience, who have been unable to find employment for a period of six months since leaving school. The duration of the programme for each participant is six months and a weekly tax-free allowance of IRL 34.50 is paid.

II
Enterprise allowance scheme: EAS

This scheme is designed to encourage unemployed people both over and under 25 years of age, to establish a business of their own. The scheme provides, for a maximum of 52 weeks, IRL 30 per week to single persons and IRL 50 per week to married persons who forego their unemployment benefit/assistance to set up their own enterprise. Applications are accepted from persons who have been a minimum of 13 weeks on the unemployment register or who are participating in AnCO training programmes.

III
Teamwork

Grants are paid mainly to local committees and groups to employ young unemployed people, under 25, on desirable community works (other than those of a major construction nature). Grants for labour will be paid at the rates prevailing locally for work of a similar nature, subject to a maximum grant of IRL 70 per week gross wages in respect of each eligible person. A grant of IRL 105 per week may also be paid towards the cost of supervision.

AnCO

I
Apprentice courses

These courses in areas such as construction, engineering, metal electrical and motor, furniture, printing and dental craftsman cater for apprentices who are sponsored by their companies or by AnCO. The appropriate normal wage for first-year apprentices is paid. When they have completed their first year with AnCO, the apprentices then resume their training in industry and qualify in the normal way.

II
Adult courses

These courses for persons aged 16 or over who have left school, are selected to meet local industrial and commercial needs and to provide the greatest chance of a job after training. AnCO, through its training centres and by utilizing suitable external training facilities, provides a comprehensive range of training opportunities for unemployed workers, redundant workers, workers leaving the land, workers wishing to up-date their skills, workers who need to change careers and first-time job seekers. Trainees are paid an appropriate allowance while undergoing training.

III
Community youth training programme (CYTP)

The AnCO CYTP was set up to provide training for young people aged between 16

and 25 years of age who have registered for employment with the National Manpower Service. Involvement in this programme should enhance the trainees' prospects of employment and help to improve confidence and self-reliance. The programme can be of real benefit by helping community groups to carry out projects aimed at improving local amenities and services. AnCO will accept for consideration projects from any community group which is non-commercial and which represents community interests. The appropriate weekly rate is paid to all participants.

IV
Community training workshops

These workshops provide basic training for young people at risk due to poor educational attainments and for travelling people. The programmes involve life skills development in addition to training in technical skills. The workshop is organized and installed in a community, by that community, with financial and technical assistance provided by AnCO and the VEC.

CERT

I
Full-time craft courses

These courses provide training for school-leavers in bar, housekeeping, kitchen, dining-room and reception skills. In Cork such courses are located at the regional technical college.

II
Preliminary courses

These courses prepare young people under the age of 18 years for full-time CERT courses.

All participants on CERT courses are paid a weekly training allowance in accordance with a set scale which is reviewed periodically.

Youth Employment Agency

I
Community enterprise programme

This programme offers a range of assistance to local groups with an approved project. The main headings of assistance are:
(i) grants of up to IRL 2 000 to assist in the sourcing/feasibility testing of ideas for products and services;
(ii) grants of up to IRL 2 000 to assist in organization development expenses;
(iii) grants of up to IRL 17 500 to assist groups to develop business ideas to point of start up;
(iv) grant aid for management grants and as a contribution towards start-up costs.

II
Youth self-employment programme

This programme, targeted at unemployed young people who have a business idea that could provide them with full-time employment, is administered in conjunction with the Bank of Ireland, who offer loans of up to IRL 3 000 per person. Applicants must be unemployed for three months and under 25 years of age.

General considerations

Within the project area the problems and difficulties facing young people in the complex transition from school to adult and working life are being tackled by a variety of education, training and work experience initiatives. There exists a complex and evolving framework of objectives, principles, perceptions of need and a wide range of ideas as to how best this transition process should be dealt with. Outlined below are some of the broad considerations which relate to the current provision.

● There is a growing emphasis on the need to provide a structured and comprehensive system of provision for young people.

● There is an emphasis on the disadvantaged including those leaving second level education without qualifications or vocational preparation and other minority groups such as the teenage travellers.

● There is clearly a desire to strengthen and reform the traditional system of education as well as pursuing 'special' innovatory programmes for the young employed.

● A growing awareness exists of the need to understand the local economy and labour market. The benefit of linking the needs of young people with the social and economic needs of the community through training and job creation are readily acknowledged.

● There is a concern for the effective use of resources in what is a complex and rapidly evolving network of objectives, providers, options and funding.

The future

The problem of the multiplicity of agencies operating at both national and local level has been of considerable concern to the Irish Government for some time past and has given rise to a number of new developments, including the following, with the intention of providing a more effective delivery of training and work preparation services for young people.

1.
At the beginning of 1984 a Minister of State was appointed to both the Ministers for Education and Labour and his report has resulted in a set of decisions agreed by the two ministers concerned which are aimed at bringing about much greater coordination of the activities of the two departments. The implementation of these decisions has just commenced and this should lead to a clearer definition of the functions of the many agencies involved, an elimination of unnecessary duplication and overlapping, and much improved cooperation between them.[1]

2.
Arising from the government's overall economic and social plan for the period to 1987 a decision was taken to establish, as a pilot scheme, eight locally-based Community Training and Employment Consortia (Comtecs) for the purpose of bringing together at local level manpower and education authorities and community organizations so as to ensure improved coordination of programmes for young people. The first Comtec was established in Cork City for a two-year period which commenced in June 1985 and it is expected that a plan comprehending the activities of all the major programme providers will have been formulated for approval early in 1986.

3.
In a discussion paper — 'Partners in education', the Minister for Education has suggested that a number of broadly-based local education councils be established which would have, *inter alia,* functions in relation to the provision, planning and development of second-level education, including technical education, and in relation to the provision and coordination of youth services and the provision and coordination of training schemes for young persons in conjunction with other agencies including AnCO, CERT, NMS and YEA.

The many and varied agencies involved in the provision of programmes of training and vocational preparation for young people have been, from the point of view of the clients being served and of the agencies themselves, a major obstacle to the most effective delivery of such training and vocational preparation services for young people particularly at local level. It is a problem which is now being tackled vigorously.

[1] See also footnote on page 156.

Contact centre for education and work (COA) — Limburg, NL

Summary

The Limburg COA is part of a national network of contact centres set up on a provincial and local basis, to develop educational, training, work experience and guidance facilities for young people, and to help the providers of these services to coordinate their objectives and their activities.

Background

The Ministries of Education and Science and of Social Affairs and Employment formed 12 environmental contact centres for education and work over the period 1983-85.

Each contact centre (Contactcentrum Onderwijs Arbeid, abbreviated to COA) has the job of improving the linkages between education and work in its region, which is generally a province. Within this principal objective a number of sub-goals were formulated, namely:

● to promote systematic information-gathering on the regional labour market, regional educational facilities and the relationship between the two;

● to promote coordination of activities in the area of school, study and vocational guidance and information;

● to promote work-experience arrangements as part of study courses;

● to promote other activities relevant to improving the links between education and work;

● to advise existing organizations on ways of improving any relevant facilities for training, guidance or linking activities.

The COAs are not intended to take over any existing activities; their purpose is to bring about cooperation between existing organizations in the fields of education and employment. Apart from the objectives listed above, central government places no obligations on the COAs regarding the details of their work or how they carry it out:

activities must be determined by and geared to the regional situation.

All COAs receive a basic grant from central government as a contribution towards their total costs; it can be used among other things to finance two establishment posts. In addition many COAs also receive supplementary funding from other organizations.

COA Limburg began work in October 1983. The management board of Limburg COA includes representatives of 35 umbrella organizations in the educational, employment and intermediary fields: together they determine what concrete activities are to be carried out by the staff of the provincial COA office (generally in collaboration with one of more of the organizations represented at management level).

Unlike the other COAs, the COA Limburg is decentralized within the province. As well as the provincial management board (on which umbrella organizations are represented) and the provincial office, six local committees and offices have been established in different parts of the province. Each local committee comprises some 35 representatives of relevant educational institutions, employers, unions, and intermediary organizations. Each local committee also has one full-time staff member.

The Dutch educational system

The Dutch system includes both public (State) and private (voluntary) schools and colleges: both are funded by central government, providing the statutory conditions regarding establishment and operation are met, but the private schools are run not by the State but by voluntary or church bodies. For young people over the age of 12, general education is provided by academic secondary (VWO) schools, which provide a six-year course leading to university entry, higher general secondary (HAVO) schools (five-year course) and intermediate general secondary (MAVO) schools (four-year course).

Vocational education is provided at three levels, lower, intermediate and higher. Entry to the intermediate and higher levels is conditional on possession of the appropriate certificates (from a MAVO course for an intermediate vocational (MBO) course, and from a HAVO or MBO course for a higher vocational (HBO) course). Lower vocational education (LBO) is an alternative to academic and general education for 12-year-olds transferring from primary school: the first two years of the four-year course are entirely given up to general subjects, and in the latter two the stress shifts to pre-vocational studies.

The school-leaving age is 16 and 16-year-old school-leavers must attend part-time courses for two days each week for one further year.

Other opportunities include:

1.

courses within the apprenticeship system, with apprentices receiving practical training from their employers and job-related education at an apprentice training school;

2.

many courses in the field of adult education;

3.

retraining and additional training courses for those who are threatened with unemployment or who need extra training to maintain their levels of skill and expertise;

4.

training organized by the Ministry of Social Affairs and Employment, sometimes in collaboration with other organizations, aimed at the unemployed and those threatened with unemployment whose inadequate training or particular qualifications make it difficult for them to find work; and

5.

courses provided by employers for their own workforce.

Within the three levels of vocational education many different options are available. However, this diversity brings with it a number of problems.

Vocational education for young people is mainly provided in schools and colleges. The higher — and intermediate — level vocational courses (HBO and MBO) include periods of practical work experience, and recently work experience arrangements have been introduced, on an experimental basis, in lower vocational courses (LBO). However, it is becoming increasingly difficult to obtain work experience facilities within firms, since the necessary guidance and support requires a considerable investment in terms of time by employers. In addition many employers are unfamiliar with the content of many types of education and training, and it seems that unknown here implies unloved. Very many schools and colleges are thus faced with a shortage of work experience places for their students.

The combination of an increasing need for education and training and the right to establish schools and colleges for which Dutch law provides has led to a considerable growth in the number of places in educational institutions. Falling rolls mean that the system is now faced with overcapacity, and it is having difficulty in adapting to the new situation.

Since vocational education (notably within the HBO and MBO sectors) for young people aged from 16-17 is mainly provided within schools and colleges, students spend long periods in the school situation being prepared for the practical work to come. This factor, and the poor employment prospects at the end of the course, mean that more and more young people are abandoning their training or deciding, when they complete their general secondary education, not to enter training. Such young people — education dropouts — are in an extremely vulnerable position on the labour market.

Under the Dutch education system anyone with sufficient qualifications can enter any form of education or training and take any vocational course he or she wishes. In practice, however, persons from the lower socioeconomic groups are concentrated in the lower forms of education. As larger numbers of young people obtain qualifications of one type or another, those with little or no vocational training find themselves in a very precarious position on the labour market. Given the similar pattern of distribution of unemployment, many families are now faced with a second generation of unemployed members.

Because vocational education is very largely concentrated in, and provided under the auspices of, schools and colleges, direct contact between training and the future jobs market has been to a great extent lost. Since educational institutions can decide for themselves whether and to what extent they respond to developments in society, a situation has arisen in which many training courses are no longer adequately geared to practical requirements. This leads to dissatisfaction on the part of employers and means that students on work experience or young people in a job find themselves faced with very different situations from those they had expected.

A further factor is the social insurance system: with few exceptions, those receiving education or training within the normal system either are not paid at all or receive a study grant (in the case of higher vocational and university courses). By abandoning education or training after the age of 18 the young person becomes eligible for some form of benefit.

Activities and target group

The work of the provincial and local COAs in Limburg falls into two categories:

1.
general activities concerned with the creation of appropriate conditions (research into problems affecting the supply of work experience places, the provision of information to employers on requirements regarding work experience within the various forms of education, the provision of information to schools and colleges on employers' needs and wishes, research relating to study, schooling and vocational choice in Limburg, etc.);

2.
specific activities (the organization of lessons and lectures by members of firms' workforce and staff, holiday courses for pupils and students aimed at familiarizing them with the world of work, symposia and meetings on particular subjects, periods of work experience for teachers, etc.).

More concretely, the general activities are concerned with the interactions of education and employment as a system, while the specific activities are directed towards particular groups of people. However, all activities are directly aimed at giving young people a better preparation for their future work and life.

In view of the background situation it is not enough to organize activities for young people alone: much of the work of preparation is carried out by adults (generally in a school situation), and improving this preparation thus implies improving the conditions under which it takes place; hence the division into general and specific activities.

This work is conditioned by three underlying difficulties:

(1)
The enormous variety of provisions for young people, bringing with it the difficulties of organizing cooperation between different local agencies, a task made even more complex by the fact that many of them are involved with different ministries at a national level.

(2)
The long-standing absence of cooperation between schools and industry (particularly small and medium-sized enterprises) makes it difficult to ensure that vocational courses are properly linked to industrial reality, and especially hard to see to it that they contain the opportunity for good work experience.

(3)
Difficulty in motivating both young people themselves, and also those who can improve their preparation for work and life. Young people are doubtful of the value of training. Teachers do not always believe it is their job to make links with employers. Employers sometimes withdraw from active participation because of some bad experience with young people in work experience.

In Limburg, as in other parts of the country, there has been a sharp increase in youth unemployment over the past 10 years. Nationally the proportion of under-25s in the unemployed population as a whole in 1982 was 45%; the figure for Limburg was three percentage points higher. Virtually all types of school and college are to be found within Limburg's educational system, and there are approaching 45 000 firms and other institutions in the province which constitute the market for young people's labour. Employers want adequately trained workers capable of flexible deployment: educational institutions can respond to this need only if they have a clear picture of the current and future structure of jobs and occupations. At both the provincial and local level COA Limburg seeks to bring the two sides together in consultations aimed at defining concrete needs and identifying problems. Solutions are then sought through the promotion of cooperation between various relevant organization.

COA Limburg currently includes representatives of:

- all trades unions and employers' organizations and young workers' associations,
- Limburg Provincial Council,
- Limburg Manpower Services (including the local employment offices and Adult Training Centres),
- Regional Apprentice Training Body for Limburg,
- associations of independent careers counsellors,
- the Open University,
- the Secondary Education Inspectorate,
- Catholic educational and training organizations,
- the information for school-leavers projects,
- school and vocational guidance institutions,
- Chambers of Commerce and Industry,
- associations of governors of educational institutions,
- Economic and Technological Institute for Limburg,
- the Netherlands Association for Personnel Policy,
- the Limburg Women's Council.

In addition the local committees include representatives of schools and larger firms, and many schools and firms cooperate with activities on an *ad hoc* or regular basis, depending on their needs and capacities.
COA Limburg has no power to compel cooperation; its activities therefore take the form of support, advice and coordination on a voluntary basis.

Sussex Training (West) — Chichester, UK

Summary

Sussex Training (West) is a consortium established to ensure that the widest possible range of local employers involve themselves in providing training for young people under the government's Youth Training Scheme (YTS).

The initiative was promoted by, and is run from, the Chichester College of Technology, and is financed by the Manpower Services Commission (MSC).

The consortium covers South-West Sussex, and includes representatives of all social partners.

Background

Chichester has a population of 23 500, and South-west Sussex 250 000.

The College of Technology is one of several which serve the county of West Sussex. It is under the direct control of the Education Department of the West Sussex County Council. Sussex Training (West) has been set up as an independent limited company with a board of 20 directors representing both trade unions and employers, and including, as *ex-officio* members, the Principal and the Vice-Principal of the Chichester College of Technology, and the Area Careers Officer for Chichester. In addition, the Head of the General vocational preparation department at the college is the Company Secretary.

The company, which has been appointed a managing agency under the Youth Training Scheme, is administered from the College of Technology.

In 1983/84 the first full year of the Youth Training Scheme, Sussex Training (West) provided training places for 208 young people, of whom 92% subsequently found jobs within the year.

In 1984/85 340 training places were provided, and it was anticipated that some 90% would move into full-time jobs during the year.

Although West Sussex is among the best areas of the UK for employment, some 25% of young people in the Chichester area were unemployed before Sussex Training (West) and other local managing agents began to operate the Youth Training Scheme (YTS). In Chichester and West Sussex as a whole there was very little youth unemployment by the end of the second year of operation of YTS.

The YTS itself has been developed as a national scheme of vocational preparation and basic training on offer to 16 year-olds and many 17 year-olds. The scheme is tightly regulated in terms of its content and its finances at a national level, but is delivered locally by sponsors, not by the Manpower Services Commission itself. In this way it is intended to reflect local labour market conditions and opportunities. Since much of the scheme is based on employers' premises, it has some of the features of a first-year apprenticeship.

At its origin YTS was divided into two sections: one called Mode A and the other Mode B.

Mode A was 80% of the whole scheme, and was employer-based. Mode B was delivered by educational and training institutions, by local authorities, voluntary organizations or other sponsors of individual training workshops, information technology centres or community projects.

In Mode B the training was provided by institutions or organizations capable of setting up programmes which confirm with MSC's rules and guidelines. MSC retain overall management responsibility for standards and quality, and controls finance very strictly.

At the time of writing YTS was being developed into a scheme to provide a two-year training for young people, and the distinctions between the two modes were being discontinued. Higher payments were being reserved for those providing training for young people whose difficulties prevent them from training with employers in the usual way. This development, alongside measures to ensure a higher and more consistent quality of training, and more extensive certification of achievement, contributes to the achievement, through YTS, of a new system of basic vocational training for young people.

All young people taking part in YTS are expected to receive the same basic elements of training. All trainees receive the same weekly training allowance of UKL 27.00 per week. Young workers in YTS receive the agreed wage for their age and occupation.

The Sussex Training (West) takes a consortium approach to providing the widest range of training to young people. It offers free membership to employers within the area of South-west Sussex, centring on Chichester. Associate membership is offered to employers outside that area who wish to take advantage of the company's training expertise and advice, and are unable to find this in their own localities.

Members who provide training places under YTS contribute a sum of UKL 100 per place per annum towards the cost of off-the-job training and monitoring. In return for this the consortium provides administration, monitoring of training, and a package of off-the-job training for each trainee. Employers themselves then have to provide a minimum of six months and a maximum of nine months of on-the-job work experience.

The consortium can offer training programmes which include the following skills:

clerical	legal and professional
computing	motor vehicle
electronics	plastics
engineering	retail & warehousing
hotel and catering	secretarial

Methods and content of training

Sussex Training (West) is founded on the principle that young people will make a better transition from school to work if they receive up to a year of foundation training, basic education and work experience, and that where possible this is best provided by employers in collaboration with other social partners who can contribute off-the-job training and information, guidance and counselling.

Young people taking part in training provided by the consortium must follow courses which conform to the MSC's national content and standards:

Basic skills	— numeracy, communication and manual, problem solving and computer skills;
World outside employment	— work and the community, and using skills for the good of the community;
World of work	— industrial practices, institutions, unions and working together;
Job-specific and broadly related skills	— skills for a particular job, related skills and transfer of skills;
Personal effectiveness	— problem-solving, planning, interpersonal skills and self-organization;
Skill transfer	— developing flexibility, adaptability and transferability of skills.

This must involve:

Induction	— Probably concentrated into an initial week — includes purpose of scheme, structure, pay, hours, rules, rights and emergency and health and safety procedures.
Occupationally-based training	— An introductory training in skills relating to one or more of the occupational training families. Should be a written programme: list of learning objectives, name of responsible supervisor, statement about where training will take place, and how it will be done. Emphasis on training through practical assignments, and ways of improving literacy and numeracy on the job.
Core areas	— Literacy, numeracy, problem-solving, manual dexterity, computer literacy and information technology.
Off-the-job training	— Minimum of 13 weeks

Can be delivered in:
— single block (full time),
— a number of shorter blocks,
— day release,
— combination of any above.
Should be integrated with rest of course. Can be provided by sponsor or contracted out to further education college, youth or-

ganization, Skillcentre, or private contractor. (Includes life and social skills training.)

Planned work experience
— Must provide specified learning opportunities.
Should be linked to off-the-job training.

Guidance and support
— Should be a named person to whom each trainee relates, concerned with trainee's development, any personal problems, future work prospects and interests outside work.

Assessment
— Carried out by a competent adult with each trainee.
Charts learning needs, potential and progress.

Review, recording and certification
— A continuous process conducted by each young person and a competent adult. The end product is a certificate or profile of what has been achieved. Must be negotiated with the trainee. Belongs to the trainee.
Should cover levels of attainment in core areas, and in specific skills. Should also record all experience gained during the year.

Range of training opportunities

The consortium's range of opportunities is governed by the employers who come forward to offer places. During the first two years these have enabled trainees to select, among others, from:

clerical
computing
electronics
engineering
hotel and catering

legal and professional
motor vehicle
plastics
retail & warehousing
secretarial

These have been backed up by a wide range of off-the-job course elements provided by the Chichester College of Technology. These have included:

clerical, secretarial and general office duties
the legal profession
computing and data processing
retail and distribution
warehousing and distribution
hotel accommodation and reception
catering and food service
hairdressing
industrial sewing and upholstery
carpentry, furniture making and restoration
factory assembly
general labouring
engineering craft
engineering technician
maintenance (electro-mechanical engineering)
electronics assembly
electronics technicians
motor vehicle servicing
motor vehicle fast change
polymer technicians
construction technicians
construction craft skills (bricklaying)
construction craft skills (carpentry & joinery)
construction craft skills (painting & decorating)
construction craft skills (plumbing)
construction office work
construction general building operatives
community care
leisure and recreation industry.

Young people in Sussex Training (West)

Sussex Training emphasize that an important objective of all that they do is to make young people self-reliant, and therefore better able to organize their participation in adult and working life. The following elements are important:

● Each trainee has a bank account opened, receives a cheque book, and has his or her weekly allowance paid into it.
● Trainees must complete and return each week their own attendance and travel records.

● As in other YTS schemes, young people who are absent without cause, persist in late arriving, or whose work is unacceptable have reductions made to their training allowances.

The Sussex Training (West) board of directors

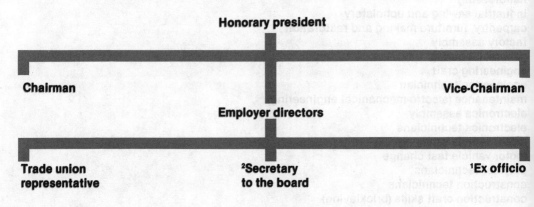

Honorary president

Chairman   Vice-Chairman

Employer directors

Trade union   ²Secretary   ¹Ex officio
representative   to the board

The District Manager of the Manpower Services Commission attends the board meetings as an observer.

¹ Ex-officio members of Sussex Training comprise:
  (1) The Principal of Chichester College of Technology,
  (2) The Vice-Principal of Chichester College of Technology,
  (3) The Area Careers Officer — Chichester.
² The Secretary to the board is also the Head of the General Vocational Preparation Department at Chichester College of Technology.

Sussex Training (West) approach to local coordination

Sussex Training (West) is an independent company limited by guarantee, and is therefore controlled by a board of directors who, legally, are the company. The majority of directors are employers drawn from those who provide training oportunities for young people, and other board members represent the Chichester College of Technology, which provides the administration of the consortium, and which also provides off-the-job training for the young people, the trades unions and the area Careers Service (which is a part of local authority). The Manpower Services Commission is included in an observer status.

Employers are recruited to the scheme partly by word of mouth from other employers, partly from the MSC local office or from the careers service. They are then recommended to Sussex Training, and are visited by staff.

Young people are recruited largely through the careers service. Some are referred directly by employers who want them included in the scheme.

Young people are then matched with the opportunities offered by the employers who are members of Sussex Training. If the training they want is not available from within the scheme, every effort is made to find them training with other appropriate employers.

Young people who are training on the job with employers are regularly visited by Sussex Training staff to ensure that everything is going according to plan. Each young person is also visited once a year by a careers officer who is concerned both with giving advice about employment prospects, and also with the quality of the training and the conditions under which it is being carried out. Regular visits are also made by MSC staff monitoring the content, the quality and the conditions of the training.

Marketing Sussex Training (West)

A major factor in the local success of a consortium like Sussex Training is the extent to which it is recognized by employers and by young people and their parents as a good basis for working life.

This has been done through:

● personal visits to employers;
● advertising aimed at young people in local newspapers, or buses, and on local radio;
● posters and brochures distributed to schools, community centres and youth clubs;
● briefing meetings for young people and their parents.

2. Further reading

Products of the European Communities' second transition programme

The following brief lists of bibliographical material have been supplied by members of the working group. They make no attempt to be exhaustive. Those who wish to have more information concerning material available in foreign countries on this theme are invited to make contact with Cedefop's library and documentation service.

Publication	Author/source
Transition	Ifaplan Square Ambiorix 32 B-1040 Brussels
Information note November 1985	
An introduction to the second action programme and its pilot projects	
Languages: All Community inc. Spanish (ES) and Portuguese (PT)	Ifaplan Square Ambiorix 32 B-1040 Brussels
Doc: 021N85	
Interim report November 1985	Ifaplan Square Ambiorix 32 B-1040 Brussels
A thematic description of the development of the second action programme after two years	
Languages: All Community **except** ES and PT	
Doc: 33WD85	
Action handbook October 1985	
How to implement gender equality	
Languages: All Community inc. ES and PT	
Doc: 05WD85	

Danish material

Uddannelsesnøglen	Nøgleforlaget Kolding
Erhvervsnøglen	Nøgleforlaget Kolding
Uddannelsessystemet	Nøgleforlaget Kolding
En vurdering af beskæftigelsesmulighederne i forskellige brancher	Amts arbejdsmarkedsnævnet
Teknologiforståelse	S.E.L.
Arbejdsmarkedsnyt	Kroghs skolehåndbog, Vejle
Erhvervskartotek	Arbejdsdirektoratet
Arbejdsmarkedet — hvad sker der	Forlaget Fremad
Fagre elektroniske verden	Forlaget Fremad
Sådan søger du job	Studie og erhverv
Vejledning	Studie og erhverv
Mit uddannelses- og erhvervsvalg	Studie og erhverv
Arbejdsmarkedets håndbog	A.O.F.
Sådan gjorde vi	Dansk arbejdsgiverforening
Idékatalog — lære/praktikpladser	Dansk arbejdsgiverforening
EFG efter basisåret	Ole Camåe
Rådgivning og vejledning i skolen	Gyldendal
Ungdomsuddannelserne og samfundet	Gyldendal
Kønsroller og vejledning	Erhvervsvejledningsrådet
Samtalen — nøglen til jobbet	Søren Hempel Ålborg
Rapport for opsøgende arbejde i Randers området 1981, 1982, 1983, 1984, 1985	Handelsskolen i Randers og Teknisk skole i Randers

German material

Die Alternativen der Alternativbewegung	IMSF	Marxistische Blätter Frankfurt 1985
Berufsbildung selber organisieren	Damm/Müller Rottmann	Jugend u. Politik Reinheim
Meine Rechte und Pflichten als Arbeitsloser	Hermann Hummel — Lilijegren	HC Beck, München
Arbeitslosigkeit	Horst Friedrich Ute Brauer	Leske u. Buderich, Opladen
Die neue Armut	Balsen/Nalielski Rössel/Winkel	Bund Verlag, Köln
Berufsausbildung? Na klar!	H. J. Petzold	BMBW
Sozialpädagogisch orientiert	W. Egler/U. Gintzel	Institut für soziale Arbeit e. V.
Die soziale Situation	DGB — Jugend NRW	DGB
Qualifizierte Ausbildung für alle	DGB — Jugend NRW	DGB
Alternative Projekte der Jugendhilfe in Berlin/Materialien	Soz. päd. Inst. W. May	Arbeiterwohlfahrt Bundesverband
Alternative Projekte der Jugendhilfe in Berlin/Endbericht	Soz. päd. Inst. W. May	Arbeiterwohlfahrt Bundesverband
Alternativbewegung Jugendprotest Selbsthilfe	E. Jordan/D. Kreft	Institut für soziale Arbeit Sozialpäd. Institut Berlin
Arbeitslosenleitfaden	Walter May	Sozialpäd. Institut Berlin
Arbeitsplätze selber schaffen	H.Bischoff/D. Damm	Biedersytein
Alternative Ausbildungs- und Arbeitsprojekte für junge Arbeitslose	Jonas/Stötzner/Pongraz	DPWV
Lebensbedingungen junger Arbeitnehmer	Braun/Schäfer/Schneider	Deutsches Jugendinstitut
Der Schatz im Silbersee	Esche/Sonthauß	Stattbuch Verlag Berlin
Unter Geiern	Arbeitsgruppe	Stattbuch Verlag Berlin
Arbeitslose — Protest und Bewegung	IMSF	Marxistische Blätter
Arbeitslos — Betroffene erzählen	Christiane Rumpeltes	RoRoRo
Geschichte der Arbeitslosigkeit	Frank Niess	Pahl-Rugenstein
Jugend ohne Arbeit	Arno Giesbrecht	Diesterweg/Sauerländer
Weg von der Straße für ein Jahr …	Walter Hanesch Uli Single	Focus Verlag
Qual ohne Wahl	Hans-Joachim Petzold Wolfgang Schlegel	Jugend & Politik
Ausbildungsverzicht — Ausbildungsabbruch — Ausbildungsversagen	Gerhard P. Bunk	Peter D. Lang

Berufseingliederung und Berufsausbildung Jugendlicher ohne Hauptschulabschluß	BIBB	BIBB
Jugendarbeitslosigkeit und soziale Sicherung	Heinrich v. d. Haar Elke Stark — v. d. Haar	Die Arbeitswelt
Ausbildungs- und Berufsstartprobleme von Jugendlichen	SOFI	SOFI
Leitfaden für Arbeitslose	Arbeitslosenprojekt TUWAS	Fachhochschule Frankfurt
Alternative Projekte der Jugendhilfe in Berlin	Arbeiterwohlfahrt Bundesverband e. V.	Arbeiterwohlfahrt Bundesverband e. V.
Die Werkschule — Berichte und Erfahrungen	Autorenkollektiv: Die Werkschulen	Werkschule Berlin Eigenverlag
Arbeitsplätze selber schaffen, finanzieren und behalten	Bischoff/Damm	Beck Verlag
Arbeit schaffen — jetzt	Bolle/Grottian	Beck Verlag
Berufsausbildung selber gemacht	Damm/Müller/Rottmann	Jugend & Politik
Gewerkschaftsjugend und Alternativbewegung	DGB Jugend	DGB
Keine Lehrstelle — was tun?	Jan Kressin	Freitag Verlag

Greek material — A variety of material is available from the following sources:

General Secretariat for Youth
(Mr Lagos)

25 Panepistimiou st., TK 10564

General Secretariat for Adult Education
(Mr Stamatakos)

56 Ermou st., TK 10563

Workforce Employment Organization (OAED)

8 Thrakis st., Trahones Attikis

Centre for Technical Studies and Training
(KEMETE Mr Apostolides)

2 Feron st., TK 10434

Mr Stavros Stavrou
(Lecturer in the University of Thessaloniki)

14 Ethnikis Aminis st., TK 54621

National Organization for Small and Medium-Sized
Manufacturers (EOMMEX)

16 Xenias st., TK 11528

Greek Industry Association

5 Xenofontos st., TK 10557

Industrial and Vocational Training Institute
(IBEPE — Mr Markopoulos)

Karamali and Dekelias st., TK 13671

Technological Research Institute (ITE)

56 Syngrou st., TK 11742

Greek Productivity Centre (Elkepa)

28 Kapodistriou st., TK 10682

Ministry of Agriculture
Agricultural Education and Information Directorate
(Mr Vroghistinos)

22 Menandrou st., TK 10552

Study and Self-Education Centre (KEMEA)

17 Aghias Filotheis st., TK 10556

Institute of Pedagogics
(Mr Stamatis Paleokrassas,
Mrs Koula Kassamati)

396 Mesoghion st., TK 15341

Vocational Orientation
(Mr Konstantinos Markopoulos)

6 Mantzarou st., TK 10672

Ministry of Education
Integrated Schools
Directorate
(Mr Kalofolias)

15 Mitropoleos st., TK 10557

Directorate for Vocational Training Programmes
Application and Studies
(Mr Hatziefstratiou)

15 Mitropoleos st., TK 10557

French material

Dossier Jeunes — 1985

Centre INFFO, Tour Europe, Cedex 07,
92080 Paris - La Défense

16-18 ans
Instruments pour l'action
Sept. 1982

Courrier de l'ADEP No 59, ADEP,
Le Central, La Courtine Mont d'Est
93160 Noisy le Grand

Avoir 20 ans dans les quartiers
Avril 1982

ADEP

Jeunes sans qualification
3 années d'opérations pilotes
Juin 1982

ADEP

Observation et évaluation du dispositif de formation
16-18 ans - Juin 1983

ADEP

L'insertion professionnelle et sociale des jeunes
1981

B. Schwartz
Rapport au Premier ministre
La Documentation Française

Guide pratique pour la création d'un centre de formation
modulaire et interinstitutionnel — 1986

Centre Expérimental de Formation
39, ave de Rochetaille
42100 Saint-Etienne

Si elles changeaient de métier?
1985

Mission Locale de la Rochelle
15, rue des Fonderies
17000 La Rochelle

Netherlands material

Arbeidsprojecten voor jongeren, wat zeggen zij er zelf van?

Instituut voor Sociaal Wetenschappelijk Onderzoek, 1985.

Kijk eens rond kwartaal

Stichting Sociaal Culturele Aktiviteiten Werklozen, 1985.

Op weg naar een gezamelijke verantwoordlijkheid, verslag van het Open Overleg Wagner

Ministerie van Onderwijs en Wetenschappen 1985

Randgroepjongeren

Ministerie van Ondewijs en Wetenschappen 1984

Sociaal Pedagogische visie op het jeugdbeleid

Bert van der Linden, 1984

Van school naar werk

Sociaal Cultureel Planbureau, 1983

Werk en de jeugd

Drs. Th. Jonkergouw, 1979

De relatie tussen beroepsonderwijs en arbeid met het oog op herindustrialisatie en bestrijding van de jeugdwerkloosheid

Pedagogisch Centrum Beroepsonderwijs Bedrijfsleven, 1983

Het kort-KMBO tussen aanbod en vraag

J. Geurts en Th. Hovels, 1982

Werkend leren in de elektrotechniek

Meijer, Buurke en de Vries, 1983

Leren werken

R. Bronneman-Helmers, 1984

Van school naar werk, educatieve voorzieningen voor jongeren met weinig opleiding

R. Bronneman-Helmers, 1983

Onderwijs en arbeid

J. Geurts, Th. de Keulenaar en J. Penders, 1983

School-leavers; educational measures

J. P. H. Sanders, 1982

Handleiding voor het voorbereiden van praktijkgerichte onderwijsprojecten

Stichting uitvoeringsgroep streekcentra, 1979.

UK material

NTI: A consultative document	Manpower Services Commission, 1981
Youth task group report	Manpower Services Commission, April 1982
ABC in action	FEU, September 1981
Vocational preparation	FEU, January 1981
Experience reflection learning	FEU, April 1978 (reprinted 1981)
Supporting YTS	FEU, 1st edition May 1983, 2nd edition May 1984, 3rd edition May 1985
Annual report	Manpower Services Commission, 1981/82, 1982/83, 1983/84
Review of the economy and employment	University of Warwick, Institute for Employment Research, Summer 1983; 1985 Volume I

Cedefop — European Centre for the Development of Vocational Training

Young people in transition — the local investment
Jeremy Harrison
Henry McLeish

Luxembourg: Office for Official Publications of the European Communities

1987 — 182 p. — 16.0 x 22.0 cm

ES, DE, GR, EN, FR, IT, NL

ISBN 92-825-6877-6

Catalogue number: HX-46-86-581-EN-C

Price (excluding VAT) in Luxembourg:

ECU 4   BFR 180   IRL 2.90   UKL 2.50   USD 4